PATH OF
COMPASSION

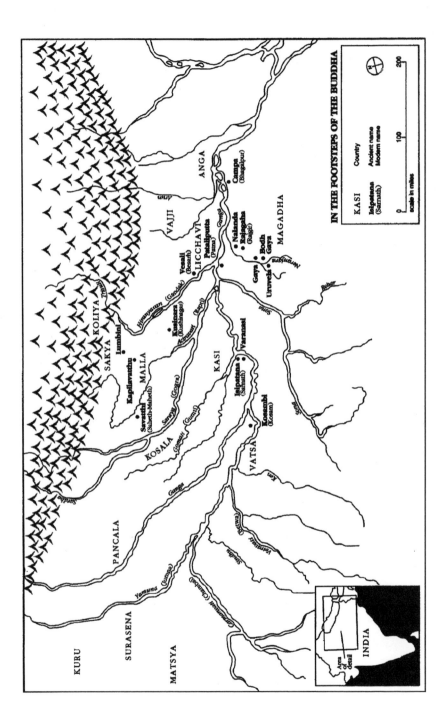

IN THE FOOTSTEPS OF THE BUDDHA

KASI   Country

Isipatana   Ancient name
(Sarnath)   Modern name

scale in miles

0   100   200

PATH OF COMPASSION

STORIES FROM THE BUDDHA'S LIFE

THICH NHAT HANH

PARALLAX PRESS / BERKELEY, CALIFORNIA

Parallax Press
P.O. Box 7355
Berkeley, California 94707
www.parallax.org

Parallax Press is the publishing division of Unified Buddhist Church, Inc.

Edited by Rachel Neumann
Drawings © 1991 by Nguyen Thi Hop and Nguyen Dong
Translated from the Vietnamese by Mobi Ho
Map by Gay Reineck
Cover and text design by Anne Nguyen

This book uses the Pali version for most people, place names, and technical
Buddhist terms, but uses the Sanskrit version of those names and terms such as
Siddhartha, Gautama, *dharma, sutra, nirvana, karma, atman,* and *bodhisattva.*

Library of Congress Cataloging-in-Publication Data
Nhât Hanh, Thích.
        [Duòng Xua Mây Trang. English]
Path of Compassion: stories from the Buddha's life/Thich Nhat Hanh; Edited
by Rachel Neumann; Translated from the Vietnamese by Mobi Ho.
        pages cm

Condensed version of: Old Path, White Clouds which is a translation of Duòng
Xua Mây Trang. Parallax Press, 1991.

ISBN 978-1-937006-13-6
1. Gautama Buddha. I. Neumann Rachel, Editor. II. Title.
BQ9800.T5392N4544513 2012
294.3'63--dc23

1 2 3 4 5 / 16 15 14 13 12

Contents

Preface

Twenty years ago, Thich Nhat Hanh wrote a book called *Old Path White Clouds* that recounted the life of the historical Buddha. The book describes the Buddha as a human being like all of us, capable of human emotions and concerns. Like the Buddha, we all have Buddha nature and are capable of living as bodhisattvas, people who have dedicated their lives to the welfare of all beings.

As Thich Nhat Hanh wrote in that original edition:

"In writing this book...I have avoided including the many miracles that are often used in the sutras to embellish the Buddha's life. The Buddha himself advised his disciples not to waste time and energy on acquiring or practicing supernatural powers. I have, however, included many of the difficulties the Buddha encountered during his life from both the larger society and his own disciples. If the Buddha appears in this book as a human being close to us, it is partly thanks to recounting such difficulties."

Since the first publication of *Old Path White Clouds*, people have requested a condensed edition of the book, focused on the Buddha's life and travels, that can introduce people to the practice of mindfulness. We created this book in the hopes that you can, indeed, carry it with you as you walk in the footsteps of the Buddha.

Rachel Neumann, Parallax Press

*As King Suddhodhana hurried in to see his wife
and newborn son, his joy was boundless.*

CHAPTER ONE

Beneath a Rose-Apple Tree

When he was nine years old, Siddhartha was told about the dream his mother had before giving birth to him. A magnificent white elephant with six tusks descended from the heavens surrounded by a chorus of beatific praises. The elephant approached his mother, its skin as white as mountain snow. It held a brilliant pink lotus flower in its trunk, and placed the flower within the queen's body. Then the elephant, too, entered her effortlessly, and all at once she was filled with deep ease and joy. She had the feeling she would never again know any suffering, worry, or pain, and she awoke uplifted by a sensation of pure bliss. When she got up from her bed, the ethereal music from the dream still echoed in her ears. She told her husband, the king, of the dream, and he, too, marveled at it. That morning, the king summoned all the holy men in the capital to come and divine the meaning of the queen's dream.

After listening intently to the dream's content, they responded, "Your majesty, the queen will give birth to a son who will be a great leader. He is destined to become either a mighty emperor who rules throughout the four directions, or a great Teacher who will show the Way of Truth to all beings in Heaven and Earth. Our land, your majesty, has long awaited the appearance of such a Great One."

King Suddhodana beamed. After consulting the queen, he ordered that provisions from the royal storehouses be distributed to the ill and unfortunate throughout the land. Thus the citizens of the kingdom of

Sakya shared the king and queen's joy over the news of their future son.

Siddhartha's mother was named Mahamaya. A woman of great virtue, her love extended to all beings—people, animals, and plants. It was the custom in those days for a woman to return to her parents' home to give birth there. Mahamaya was from the country of Koliya, so she set out for Ramagama, the capital of Koliya. Along the way, she stopped to rest in the garden of Lumbini. The forest there was filled with flowers and singing birds. Peacocks fanned their splendid tails in the morning light. Admiring an *ashok* tree in full bloom, the queen walked toward it when suddenly, feeling unsteady, she grabbed a branch of the ashok tree to support her. Just a moment later, still holding the branch, Queen Mahamaya gave birth to a radiant son.

The prince was bathed in fresh water and wrapped in yellow silk by Mahamaya's attendants. As there was no longer any need to return to Ramagama, the queen and the newborn prince were carried home in their four-horse carriage. When they arrived home, the prince was again bathed in warm water and placed next to his mother.

Hearing the news, King Suddhodana hurried in to see his wife and son. His joy was boundless. His eyes sparkled and he named the prince Siddhartha, which meant "the one who accomplishes his aim." Everyone in the palace rejoiced and, one by one, they came to offer their congratulations to the queen. King Suddhodana wasted no time in summoning the soothsayers to tell him of Siddhartha's future. After examining the baby's features, they all agreed that the boy bore the marks of a great leader and would no doubt rule over a mighty kingdom that spread in all four directions.

One week later, a holy man named Asita Kaladevala paid a visit to the palace. His back was bent with age, and he needed a cane to descend the mountain where he lived. When the palace guards announced Master Asita's arrival, King Suddhodana personally came out to greet him. He ushered him in to see the baby prince. The holy man gazed at the prince for a long time without uttering a word. Then he began to weep, his trembling body supported by his cane. Streams of tears fell from his eyes.

King Suddhodana grew alarmed and asked, "What is it? Do you forebode some misfortune for the child?"

Master Asita wiped the tears with his hands and shook his head. "Your majesty, I see no misfortune at all. I weep for myself, for I can clearly see that this child possesses true greatness. He will penetrate all the mysteries of the universe. Your majesty, your son will not be a politician. He will be a great Master of the Way. Heaven and Earth will be his home and all beings his relations. I weep because I will pass away before I have a chance to hear his voice proclaim the truths he will realize. Majesty, you and your country possess great merit to have given birth to such a one as this boy."

Asita turned to leave. The king pleaded for him to stay, but it was of no use. The old man began walking back to his mountain. Master Asita's visit sent the king into a frenzy. He did not want his son to become a monk. He wanted Siddhartha to assume his throne and extend the borders of their kingdom. The king thought, "Asita is only one among hundreds, even thousands of holy men. Perhaps his prophecy is mistaken. Surely the other holy men who said Siddhartha would become a great emperor were correct." Clinging to this hope, the king was comforted.

After having attained sublime joy giving birth to Siddhartha, Queen Mahamaya died eight days later, and all the kingdom mourned her. King Suddhodana summoned the queen's sister Mahapajapati, and asked her to become the new queen. Mahapajapati, also known as Gotami, agreed, and she cared for Siddhartha as if he were her own son. As the boy grew older and asked about his real mother, he understood how much Gotami had loved her sister and how she, more than anyone else in the world, could love him as much as his own mother. Under Gotami's care, Siddhartha grew strong and healthy.

One day, as Gotami watched Siddhartha play in the garden, she realized he was old enough to learn the graces of wearing gold and precious gems. She instructed her attendants to bring forth precious jewels to try on Siddhartha, but, to her surprise, none rendered Siddhartha more handsome than he already was. As Siddhartha expressed discomfort at wearing such things, Gotami ordered the jewels to be returned to their cases.

When Siddhartha reached school age, he studied literature, writing, music, and athletics with the other princes of the Sakya dynasty. Among his schoolmates were his cousins Devadatta and Kimbila, and the son of a palace dignitary, a boy named Kaludayi. Naturally intelligent, Siddhartha mastered his lessons quickly. His teacher Vishvamitra found the young Devadatta a sharp student, but never in his teaching career had he taught a student more impressive than Siddhartha.

When he was nine years old, Siddhartha and his schoolmates were allowed to attend the ritual first plowing of the fields. Gotami herself dressed Siddhartha, right down to the fine slippers on his feet. Attired in his royal best, King Suddhodana presided over the ceremonies. High-ranking holy men and *brahmans* paraded in robes and headdresses of every color imaginable. The ceremony was held next to the finest fields in the kingdom, not far from the palace itself. Flags and banners waved from every gate and along every roadside. Colorful displays of food and drink were laid out on altars crowded along the roads. Minstrels and musicians strolled among the throngs of people, adding mirth and merriment to the bustling festivities. Holy men chanted with utmost solemnity as Siddhartha's father and all the dignitaries of the court stood facing the unfolding ritual.

Siddhartha stood toward the back with Devadatta and Kaludayi at his sides. The boys were excited because they had been told that when the rituals were over, everyone would enjoy a feast spread out on the grassy meadow. Siddhartha did not often go on picnics and he was delighted. But the holy men's chanting went on and on for what seemed like forever, and the young boys grew restless. Unable to endure any more, they wandered off. Kaludayi held onto Siddhartha's sleeve, and off they went in the direction of the music and dancing. The hot sun blazed and the performers' costumes grew wet with perspiration. Beads of sweat shone on the dancing girls' foreheads. After running about among the scenes of entertainment, Siddhartha, too, grew hot and he left his friends to seek the shade of the rose-apple tree alongside the road. Beneath the cool branches, Siddhartha felt pleasantly refreshed. At that moment, Gotami appeared and, spotting her son, she said, "I've been looking all over for you. Where have you been? You should return now for the conclusion of the ceremony. It would please your father."

"Mother, the ceremony is too long. Why must the holy men chant so long?"

"They are reciting the Vedas, my child. The scriptures have a profound meaning, handed down by the Creator himself to the brahmans countless generations ago. You will study them soon."

"Why doesn't Father recite the scriptures instead of having the brahmans do it?"

"Only those born into the brahmana caste are permitted to recite the scriptures, my child. Even kings who wield great power must depend on the services of the brahmans for priestly duties."

Siddhartha thought over Gotami's words. After a long pause, he joined his palms and entreated her, "Please Mother, ask Father if I may stay here. I feel so happy sitting beneath this rose-apple tree."

Giving in good-naturedly to her child, Gotami smiled and nodded. She stroked his hair, and then returned down the path.

At last, the brahmans concluded their prayers. King Suddhodana stepped down into the fields and, together with two military officers, began to plow the first row of the season as cheers resounded among the crowd. Then the farmers followed the king's example and began to plow their fields. Hearing the people's cheers, Siddhartha ran to the edge of the fields. He watched a water buffalo straining to pull a heavy plow, followed by a robust farmer whose skin was bronzed from long work in the sun. The farmer's left hand steadied the plow while his right hand wielded a whip to urge the buffalo on. Sun blazed and the man's sweat poured in streams from his body. The rich earth was divided into two neat furrows. As the plow turned the earth, Siddhartha noticed that the bodies of worms and other small creatures were being cut as well. As the worms writhed upon the ground, they were spotted by birds who flew down and grabbed them in their beaks. Then Siddhartha saw a large bird swoop down and grasp a small bird in its talons.

Utterly absorbed in these events, standing beneath the burning sun, Siddhartha became drenched in sweat. He ran back to the shade of the rose-apple tree. He had just witnessed so many things strange and unknown to him. He sat cross-legged and closed his eyes to reflect on all he had seen. Composed and still he sat for a long time, oblivious to all the singing, dancing, and picnicking taking place around him. Siddhartha continued to sit, absorbed by the images of the field and the many creatures. When the king and queen passed by sometime later, they discovered Siddhartha still sitting in deep concentration. Gotami was moved to tears seeing how beautiful Siddhartha looked, like a small statue. But King Suddhodana was seized with sudden apprehension. If Siddhartha could sit so solemnly at such a young age, might not Asita's prophecy come true? Too disturbed to remain for the picnic, the king returned alone to the palace in his royal carriage.

Some poor country children passed by the tree, speaking and laughing happily. Gotami motioned them to be quiet. She pointed to Siddhartha sitting beneath the rose-apple tree. Curious, the children stared at him. Suddenly, Siddhartha opened his eyes. Seeing the queen, he smiled.

"Mother," he said, "reciting the scriptures does nothing to help the worms and the birds."

Siddhartha stood up and ran to Gotami and clasped her hand. He then noticed the children observing him. They were about his own age, but their clothes were tattered, their faces soiled, and their arms and legs piteously thin. Aware of his princely attire, Siddhartha felt embarrassed, and yet he wanted very much to play with them. He smiled and hesitantly waved, and one boy smiled back. That was all the encouragement Siddhartha needed. He asked Gotami for permission to invite the children to the picnic feast. At first she hesitated, but then she nodded in assent.

CHAPTER TWO

The Path of Compassion

When Siddhartha was fourteen years old, Queen Gotami gave birth to a son, Nanda. All the palace rejoiced, including Siddhartha, who was very happy to have a younger brother. Every day after his studies, he ran home to visit Nanda. Although Siddhartha was already of an age to be concerned with other matters, he often took little Nanda on walks, accompanied by his cousin Devadatta.

Siddhartha had three other cousins that he liked very much, named Mahanama, Baddhiya, and Kimbila. He often invited them to play with him in the flower garden behind the palace. With each passing year, Siddhartha grew ever more adept in his studies and Devadatta had a hard time concealing his jealousy. Siddhartha mastered every subject with ease, including the martial arts. He was brilliant in math and was especially gifted in music. On summer evenings he liked to sit alone in the garden and play the flute given to him by his music teacher.

Siddhartha concentrated intensely in his religious and philosophical studies. He was instructed in all the Vedas, and he pondered the meanings of the teachings and beliefs they expounded. His teachers wanted only to instruct their charges in the traditional beliefs, but Siddhartha and his companions insisted on asking questions that forced their teachers to address contemporary ideas that did not always seem to accord with tradition.

On the days the boys were off from school, Siddhartha persuaded them to visit and discuss these matters with well-known priests and brahmans in the capital. Thanks to these encounters, Siddhartha learned that there were a number of movements in the country which openly challenged the absolute authority of the brahmans. Members of these movements were not only discontented laymen who wished to share some of the power that had long belonged exclusively to the brahmana caste, but they included reform-minded members of the brahmana caste as well.

Since the day young Siddhartha had been given permission to invite a few poor country children to his royal picnic, he had also been allowed to visit, from time to time, the small villages that surrounded the capital. On these occasions, he was always careful to wear only simple garments. By speaking directly with the people, Siddhartha learned many things that he had never been exposed to in the palace. He was aware, of course, that the people served and worshipped the three deities of Brahmanism—Brahma, Vishnu, and Shiva. But he also learned that the people were manipulated and oppressed by the brahmana priests. In order to have the proper rituals for births, marriages, and funerals, families were forced to pay the brahmans in food, money, and physical labor, regardless of how impoverished they were.

As a result of his own reflections, Siddhartha began to question some of the fundamental teachings of Brahmanism: why had the Vedas been given exclusively to the brahmana caste, why was Brahman the Supreme Ruler of the universe, and what was the omnipotent power that prayers and rituals possessed. Siddhartha sympathized with those priests and brahmans who dared to directly challenge these dogmas. His interest never waned, and Siddhartha never missed a class or discussion on the Vedas. He also pursued the studies of language and history.

Siddhartha liked very much to meet and have discussions with hermits and monks, but as his father disapproved, he had to find excuses to go on other excursions in the hope of encountering such men. These monks cared nothing for material possessions and social status, unlike the brahmans who openly vied for power. Rather, these monks abandoned everything in order to seek liberation and to cut the ties that bound them to the sorrows and worries of the world. They were men who had studied and penetrated the meaning of the Vedas and the Upanishads. Siddhartha knew that many such hermits lived in Kosala, the neighboring kingdom to the west, and in Magadha which lay to the south. Siddhartha hoped that one day he would have a chance to visit these regions and study seriously with men such as these.

Of course, King Suddhodana was aware of Siddhartha's aspirations. He dreaded that his son might one day leave the palace and become a monk and he confided his worries to his younger brother, Dronodanaraja, the father of Devadatta and Ananda.

"The country of Kosala has long had its eye on our territory. We must count on the talents of our young people, such as Siddhartha and Devadatta, to protect the destiny of our country. I greatly fear Siddhartha may decide to become a monk. If this comes to pass, it is likely that Devadatta will follow in Siddhartha's footsteps. Do you know how much they like to go out and meet with these hermits?"

Dronodanaraja was taken aback by the king's words. After pondering a moment, he whispered in the king's ear, "I think you should find a wife for Siddhartha. Once he has a family to occupy him, he will abandon this desire to become a monk." King Suddhodana nodded.

That night he confided his concerns to Gotami, who promised she would arrange for Siddhartha to marry in the near future. Even though she had just recently given birth to a girl named Sundari Nanda, she began to organize a number of gatherings for the young people in the kingdom. Siddhartha joined these evenings of music, athletic events, and field trips with enthusiasm. He made many new friends, both young men and young women.

King Suddhodana had a younger sister, Pamita, whose husband was King Dandapani of Koliya. The couple kept residences in both Ramagama, the capital of Koliya, and in Kapilavatthu. Sakya and Koliya were separated only by the Rohini River and their peoples had been close for many generations. Their capitals were but a day's journey apart. At Gotami's request, the king and queen of Koliya agreed to organize a martial arts competition on the large field that bordered Kunau Lake. King Suddhodana personally presided over the event to encourage the young people of his kingdom to develop their strength and increase their fighting skills. All the young people of the capital were invited to attend, girls as well as boys. The young women did not engage in the athletic contests but encouraged the young men with their praise and applause. Yasodhara, the daughter of Queen Pamita and King Dandapani, was responsible for welcoming all the guests. She was a lovely and charming young woman, her beauty natural and fresh.

As he grew into his teens, Siddhartha came to find palace life stifling. He began making excursions beyond the city limits to see what life was like outside. He was always accompanied by Channa, his faithful attendant, and sometimes also by his friends or brothers. Channa and Siddhartha took turns holding the reins. As Siddhartha never used a whip, Channa did not either.

Siddhartha visited every corner of the Sakya kingdom, from the rugged foothills of the Himalayan mountains in the north to the great southern plains. The capital, Kapilavatthu, was located in the richest, most populated region of the lowlands. Compared with the neighboring kingdoms of Kosala and Magadha, Sakya was quite small, but what it lacked in area it more than made up in its ideal location. The Rohini and Banganga Rivers, which began in the highlands, flowed down to irrigate its rich plains. They continued southward and joined the Hiranyavati River before emptying into the Ganga. Siddhartha loved to sit on the banks of the Banganga and watch the water rush by.

One day, as he was returning to the palace, Siddhartha was surprised to see Yasodhara in a small, poor village, with one of her maid servants, tending to the village children who were suffering from eye diseases, influenza, skin disorders, and other ailments. Yasodhara was dressed simply, yet she appeared to be as a goddess who had appeared among the poor. Siddhartha was deeply moved to see the daughter of a royal family placing her own comfort aside so that she could care for the destitute. She rinsed their infected eyes and skin, dispensed medicine, and washed their soiled clothes.

"Princess, how long have you been doing this?" asked Siddhartha. "It is beautiful to see you here."

Yasodhara looked up from washing a little girl's arm. "For almost two years, your highness. But this is only the second time I have been in this village."

"I often stop here. The children know me well. Your work must give you a great feeling of satisfaction, princess."

Yasodhara smiled without answering. She bent over to continue washing the girl's arm.

That day, Siddhartha had a chance to speak with Yasodhara for a longer time. He was surprised to learn that she shared many of his own ideas. Yasodhara was not content to remain in her lady's quarters blindly obeying tradition. She, too, had studied the Vedas and secretly opposed society's injustices. And like Siddhartha, she did not feel truly happy being a privileged member of a wealthy royal family. She loathed the power struggles among the courtiers and even among the brahmans. She knew that as a woman she could not effect great social change, so she found ways to express her convictions through charitable work. She hoped that her friends might see the value of this through her example.

Since the day he first saw her, Siddhartha had felt a special affinity for Yasodhara. Now he found himself drawn to every word she spoke. His father had expressed a desire that he marry soon. Perhaps Yasodhara was the right woman. During the musical and athletic gatherings, Siddhartha had met many charming young women, but Yasodhara was the one with whom he felt ease and contentment.

Siddhartha and Yasodhara's wedding took place the following autumn. It was an occasion of great joy and celebration for the entire kingdom. The capital, Kapilavatthu, was decked with flags, lanterns, and flowers, and there was music everywhere. Wherever Siddhartha and Yasodhara went in their carriage, they were greeted with resounding cheers. They also visited outlying hamlets and villages, bringing gifts of food and clothing to many poor families.

*Siddhartha and Yasodhara's wedding was an occasion of great joy and
celebration for the entire kingdom.*

King Suddhodana supervised the building of three palaces for the young couple, one for each season. The summer palace was built on a beautiful hillside in the highlands, while the rainy season and winter palaces were in the capital city. King Suddhodana was at peace, now that Siddhartha had followed the path he had wished his son to follow. He personally selected the finest musicians and dancers in the kingdom to provide continual and pleasant entertainment for his young son and daughter-in-law.

But happiness for Siddhartha and Yasodhara was not to be found in a pampered life of wealth and status. Their happiness came from opening their hearts and sharing their deepest thoughts with each other. They weren't moved by exquisite and savory foods or fancy silken clothes. While they could appreciate the artistry of the dancers and musicians, they were not carried away by the pleasures they offered. They had their own dreams—to find answers concerning the spiritual quest and the renewal of society.

The following summer, as Channa drove them to their summer palace, Siddhartha introduced Yasodhara to places throughout the kingdom she did not yet know. They stayed several days at each location, sometimes spending the night in the homes of country folk, sharing their simple foods and sleeping upon their woven string beds. They learned a great deal about the way of life and the customs of each place they visited.

At times they encountered terrible misery. They met families with nine or ten children, every child racked with disease. No matter how hard the parents toiled day and night, they could not earn enough to support so many children. Hardship went hand in hand with the life of the peasants. Siddhartha gazed at children with arms and legs as thin as matchsticks and bellies swollen from worms and malnutrition. He saw the handicapped and infirm forced to beg in the streets, and these scenes robbed him of any happiness. He saw people caught in inescapable conditions. In addition to poverty and disease, they were oppressed by the brahmans, and there was no one to whom they could complain. The capital was too distant and, even if they went there, who would help them? He knew that even a king had no power to change the situation.

Siddhartha had long understood the inner workings of the royal court. Every official was intent on protecting and fortifying his own power, not on alleviating the suffering of those in need. He had seen the powerful plot against each other, and he felt nothing but revulsion for politics. He knew that even his own father's authority was fragile and restricted—a king did not possess true freedom but was imprisoned by his position. His father was aware of many officials' greed and corruption, but was forced to rely on these same individuals to maintain the stability of his reign. Siddhartha realized that if he stood in his father's place, he would have to do the same. He understood that only when people overcame greed and envy in their own hearts would conditions change. And so his desire to seek a path of spiritual liberation was reignited.

Yasodhara was bright and intuitive. She understood Siddhartha's longings, and she had faith that if Siddhartha resolved to find the path of liberation he would succeed. But she was also quite practical. Such a search could last months, even years. In the meantime, sufferings would continue to daily unfold around them. And so she believed it was important to respond right in the present moment. She discussed with Siddhartha ways to ease the suffering of the poorest members of society. She had been doing work like that for several years, and her efforts eased some of the people's misery and brought some measure of peace and happiness to her own heart as well. She believed that with Siddhartha's loving support she could continue such work for a long time.

From Kapilavatthu came pouring all manner of goods and servants to provide for the couple's summer needs. Siddhartha and Yasodhara sent home most of the servants, retaining only a few to assist them with the gardens, cooking, and housekeeping. Yasodhara organized their daily life as simply as possible. Siddhartha understood her need to engage in social action, and he never failed to express his support.

Although Siddhartha understood the value of Yasodhara's work, he felt that her path alone could not bring true peace. People were entrapped not only by illness and unjust social conditions, but by the sorrows and passions they themselves created in their own hearts and minds. And if, in time, Yasodhara fell victim to fear, anger, bitterness, or disappointment, where would she find the energy needed to continue her work? Siddhartha had himself experienced suspicion, frustration, and pain when he saw how things worked in the palace and in society. He knew that the attainment of inner peace would be the only basis for true social work, but he did not yet confide these thoughts to Yasodhara.

When the couple returned to their winter palace, they entertained a constant stream of guests. Yasodhara welcomed family members and friends with great warmth and respect, but she was most attentive when Siddhartha spoke with them about philosophy and religion, and their relation to politics and society. Even while going back and forth to direct the servants, Yasodhara never missed a word of these conversations. She had hoped to discover among their friends some who might like to join her work for the poor, but few expressed interest in such pursuits. Most were more interested in feasting and having a good time. Yet Siddhartha and Yasodhara patiently received them all.

In addition to Siddhartha, there was one other person who understood and wholeheartedly supported Yasodhara's efforts— Gotami, the Queen Mahapajapati. The queen was most attentive to her daughter-in-law's happiness, for she knew that if Yasodhara was happy, Siddhartha would be happy as well. But that was not the sole reason she supported Yasodhara's good work. Gotami was a woman of compassion and from the first time she accompanied Yasodhara on a visit to a poor village, she understood at once the true value of Yasodhara's work. It was not just the material goods given to the poor, such as rice, flour, cloth, and medicine, but the kind glances, helping hands, and loving heart of one willing to respond directly to those who suffer.

Queen Mahapajapati was not like other women in the palace. She frequently told Yasodhara that women possessed as much wisdom and strength as men and needed to shoulder the responsibilities of society also. While women did possess a special ability to create warmth and happiness in their families, there was no reason for them to remain only in the kitchen or in the palace. Gotami found in her daughter-in-law a woman with whom she could share true friendship for, like herself, Yasodhara was thoughtful and independent. Not only did the queen offer Yasodhara her approval, but she worked alongside her.

CHAPTER THREE

Unborn Child

During this time, King Suddhodana expressed the desire to have Siddhartha spend more time at his side so that he could instruct his son in political and courtly affairs. The prince was invited to attend many official meetings, sometimes alone with the king, at other times with the king's court. Siddhartha gave his full attention to these affairs, and he came to understand that the political, economic, and military problems that beset any kingdom had their roots in the selfish ambitions of those involved in politics. Concerned only with protecting their own power, it was impossible for them to create enlightened policies for the common good. When Siddhartha saw corrupt officials feign virtue and morality, anger filled his heart. But he concealed it, as he did not have any alternatives to offer.

"Why don't you contribute ideas at court instead of always sitting so silently?" King Suddhodana asked one day after a long meeting with several officials.

Siddhartha looked at his father. "It is not that I haven't ideas, but it would be useless to state them. They only point to the disease. I do not yet see a cure for the selfish ambitions of those in the court. Look at Vessamitta, for example. He holds an impressive amount of power at court, yet you know he is corrupt. More than once he has tried to encroach upon your authority, but you are still forced to depend on his services. Why? Because you know if you don't, chaos will break loose."

King Suddhodana looked at his son silently for a long moment. Then he spoke. "Siddhartha, you know well that in order to maintain peace in one's family and country, there are certain things one must tolerate. My own power is limited, but I am sure that if you prepared yourself to be king, you would do far better than I have. You possess the talent needed to purge the ranks of corruption while preventing chaos in our homeland."

Siddhartha sighed. "Father, I do not think it is a question of talent. I believe the fundamental problem is to liberate one's own heart and mind. I too am trapped by feelings of anger, jealousy, fear, and desire."

These exchanges between father and son made King Suddhodana grow increasingly anxious. He recognized that Siddhartha was a person of unusual depth, and he saw how differently he and his son viewed the world. Still, he fostered the hope that, over time, Siddhartha would come to accept his role and fill it in a most worthy way.

In addition to his duties at court and assisting Yasodhara, Siddhartha continued to meet and study with well-known brahmans and monks. He knew that the pursuit of religion was not just the study of the holy scriptures but included the practice of meditation to attain liberation for one's heart and mind, and he sought to learn more about meditation. He applied all that he learned in these studies to his own life in the palace, and he shared these insights with Yasodhara.

"Gopa," Siddhartha liked to call Yasodhara affectionately, "perhaps you should also practice meditation. It will bring peace to your heart and enable you to continue your work for a long time."

Yasodhara followed his advice. No matter how busy her work kept her, she reserved time for meditation. Husband and wife often sat together silently. At such times, their attendants left them alone, and the couple asked their musicians and dancers to go perform elsewhere.

From the time he was small, Siddhartha had been taught the four stages of a brahman's life. In youth, a brahman studied the Vedas. In the second stage, he married, raised a family, and served society. In the third stage, when his children were grown, he could retire and devote himself to religious studies. And in the fourth stage, released from every tie and obligation, a brahman could live the life of a monk. Siddhartha thought about it and concluded that by the time one was old, it would be too late to study the Way. He did not want to wait that long.

"Why can't a person live all four ways at once? Why can't a man pursue a religious life while he still has a family?"

Siddhartha wanted to study and practice the Way in the very midst of his present life. Of course, he could not refrain from thinking about famous teachers in distant places such as Savatthi or Rajagaha. He was sure that if he could find a way to study with such masters, he would make much more progress. The monks and teachers he frequently met had all mentioned the names of certain great masters such as Alara Kalama and Uddaka Ramaputta. Everyone aspired to study with such masters and each day, Siddhartha felt his own desire grow ever more urgent.

One afternoon Yasodhara came home, her face filled with grief. She did not speak to anyone. A young child she had tended for more than a week had just died. Despite all her efforts, she could not rescue the child from death's grasp. Overcome with sadness, she sat in meditation while tears streamed down her cheeks. It was impossible to hold back her feelings. When Siddhartha returned from a meeting at court, she again burst into tears. Siddhartha held her in his arms and tried to console her.

"Gopa, tomorrow I will go with you to the funeral. Cry now, it will lessen the pain in your heart. Birth, old age, sickness, and death are heavy burdens each of us carries in this life. What has happened to the child could happen to any of us at any moment."

Yasodhara spoke between sobs, "Each day, I see how true all the things you have said are. My two hands are so small compared to the immensity of suffering. My heart is constantly filled with anxiety and sorrow. O husband, please show me how I can overcome the suffering in my heart."

Siddhartha embraced Yasodhara tightly in his arms. "My wife, I myself am seeking a path to overcome the suffering and anxiety in my

Husband and wife often sat together silently.

own heart. I have seen into the situation of society and human beings but, despite all my efforts, I have not yet seen the way to liberation. Yet I feel sure that one day I will find a way for all of us. Gopa, please have faith in me."

"I have never been without faith in you, my darling. I know that once you have resolved to accomplish something, you will pursue it until you succeed. I know that one day you will leave all your wealth and privileges behind in order to seek the Way. Only, please, my husband, do not leave me just now. I need you."

Siddhartha raised Yasodhara's chin and looked into her eyes, "No, no, I won't leave you now. Only when, when..."

Yasodhara placed her hand over Siddhartha's mouth. "Siddhartha, please say no more. I want to ask you something—if you were to have a child with me, would you want it to be a boy or a girl?"

Siddhartha was startled. He looked carefully at Yasodhara. "What are you saying, Gopa? Do you mean, can you be..."

Yasodhara nodded. She pointed to her belly and said, "I am so happy to be carrying the fruit of our love. I want it to be a child who looks just like you, with your intelligence and kind virtue."

Siddhartha put his arms around Yasodhara and held her close. In the midst of his great joy, he felt the seeds of worry.

Still, he smiled and said, "I will be just as happy if it is a boy or a girl, just so long as the baby has your compassion and wisdom. Gopa, have you told Mother?"

"You are the only one I have told. This evening, I will go to the main palace and tell Queen Gotami. At the same time, I will ask her advice on how best to care for our unborn child. Tomorrow I will go tell my own mother, Queen Pamita. I'm sure everyone will be very happy."

Siddhartha nodded. He knew that his mother would pass the news on to his father as soon as she learned of it. The king would be overjoyed and would no doubt organize a great banquet to celebrate. Siddhartha felt the ties that bound him to life in the palace tightening.

Months flew by and the day for Yasodhara to give birth approached.

Queen Pamita told her daughter she did not need to return home to give birth, as Pamita herself was then living in Kapilavatthu. With Queen Mahapajapati, Pamita selected the finest midwives in the capital to assist Yasodhara. On the day Yasodhara went into labor, both Queen Gotami and Queen Pamita were there. A solemn and expectant atmosphere pervaded the palace. Although King Suddhodana did not show his presence, Siddhartha knew that the king anxiously awaited news of the birth in his own quarters.

When Yasodhara's labor pains began in earnest, she was led into the inner chamber by her attendants. It was only the noon hour, but suddenly the sky grew dark with clouds, as though a deity's hand had obscured the sun. Siddhartha sat outside. Although he was separated from his wife by two walls, he could clearly hear her cries. With each passing moment, his anxiety increased. Yasodhara's moans now followed one upon another, and he was beside himself. Her cries tore at his heart until it was impossible to sit still. He stood and paced the floor. At times Yasodhara's groans were so intense he could not quell his panic. His mother, Queen Mahamaya, had died as a result of giving birth to him, and that was a sorrow he could never forget. Now it was Yasodhara's turn to give birth to his own child. Childbirth was a passage most married women experienced, a passage fraught with danger, including the possibility of death. Sometimes both mother and child died.

Reminding himself what he had learned from a monk a number of months earlier, Siddhartha sat down in the lotus position and began to take hold of his mind and heart. This time of passage was a true test. He must maintain a calm heart even in the midst of Yasodhara's cries. Suddenly, the image of a newborn child arose in his mind. It was the image of his own child. Everyone had hoped he would have a child and would be happy for him once he did. He himself had hoped for a child. But now in the intensity of the actual event, he understood how immensely important the birth of a child is. He had not yet found his own path; he did not yet know where he was going; and yet here he was having a child—was it not a pity for the child?

Yasodhara's cries abruptly stopped. He stood up. What had happened? He could feel his own heartbeat. He observed his breath again in order to regain his calm. Just at that moment, the cries of an infant arose. The baby was born! Siddhartha wiped the sweat from his forehead.

Queen Gotami opened the door and looked in at him. She smiled and Siddhartha knew that Yasodhara was safe. The queen sat down before him and said, "Gopa has given birth to a boy."

Siddhartha smiled and looked at his mother with gratitude.

"I will name the child Rahula."

That afternoon, Siddhartha entered the room to visit his wife and son. Yasodhara gazed at him, her shining eyes filled with love. Their son lay by her side, swaddled in silk, and Siddhartha could see only his plump little face. Siddhartha looked at Yasodhara as if to ask something. Understanding, she nodded her assent and gestured for Siddhartha to pick up Rahula. Siddhartha lifted the infant in his arms as Yasodhara watched. Siddhartha felt as though he were floating, and yet his heart was heavy with worry.

Yasodhara rested for several days. Queen Gotami took care of everything from preparing special foods to tending the fireplace to keep mother and child warm. One day after they returned home, Siddhartha visited his wife and son, and as he held Rahula in his arms, he marveled at how precious and fragile a human life was. He recalled the day he and Yasodhara had attended the funeral of a poor child, four years old. Siddhartha handed Rahula back to Yasodhara. He went outside and sat alone in the garden until the evening shadows fell.

After preparing Kanthaka for a long journey, Channa asked Siddhartha,
"May I accompany you?"

CHAPTER FOUR

Kanthaka

Yasodhara quickly regained her strength and soon was able to return to her work, while also spending much time with baby Rahula. One spring day, at Queen Gotami's insistence, Channa drove Siddhartha and Yasodhara out into the countryside for an outing. They brought Rahula along and a young servant girl named Ratna to help care for him. Pleasant sunlight streamed down upon tender green leaves. Birds sang on the blossoming branches of ashok and rose-apple trees. Channa let the horses trot at a leisurely pace. Country folk, recognizing Siddhartha and Yasodhara, stood and waved in greeting. When they approached the banks of the Banganga River, Channa pulled on the reins and brought the carriage to a sudden halt. Blocking the road before them was a man who had collapsed. His arms and legs were pulled in toward his chest and his whole body shook. Moans escaped from his half-open mouth. Siddhartha jumped down, followed by Channa. The man lying in the road looked less than thirty years old. Siddhartha picked up his hand and said to Channa, "It looks as though he's come down with a bad flu, don't you think? Let's massage him and see if it helps."

Channa shook his head. "Your highness, these aren't the symptoms of a bad flu. I'm afraid he's contracted something far worse—this is a disease for which there is no known cure."

"Are you sure?" Siddhartha gazed at the man. "Couldn't we take him to the royal physician?"

"Your highness, even the royal physician can't cure this disease. I've heard this disease is highly infectious. If we take him in our carriage, he might infect your wife and son, and even yourself. Please, your highness, for your own safety, let go of his hand."

But Siddhartha did not release the man's hand—he looked at it and then at his own. Siddhartha had always enjoyed good health, but now looking at the dying man no older than himself, all he had taken for granted suddenly vanished. From the riverbank came cries of mourning. He looked up to see a funeral taking place. There was the funeral pyre. The sound of chanting intertwined with the grief-stricken cries and the crackling of fire as the funeral pyre was lit.

Looking again at the man, Siddhartha saw that he had stopped breathing. His glassy eyes stared upward. Siddhartha released his hand and quietly closed the eyes. When Siddhartha stood up, Yasodhara was standing close behind him. How long she had been there, he did not know.

She spoke softly, "Please, my husband, go and wash your hands in the river. Channa, you do the same. Then we will drive into the next village and notify the authorities so they can take care of the body."

Afterward, no one had the heart to continue their spring outing. Siddhartha asked Channa to turn around, and on the way back no one spoke a word.

That night, Yasodhara's sleep was disturbed by three strange dreams. In the first, she saw a white cow on whose head was a sparkling jewel, as bright as the North Star. The cow strolled through Kapilavatthu headed for the city gates. From the altar of Indra resounded a divine voice, "If you can't keep this cow, there will be no light left in all the capital." Everyone in the city began chasing after the cow yet no one was able to detain it. It walked out the city gates and disappeared.

In her second dream, Yasodhara watched four god-kings of the skies, atop Mount Sumeru, projecting a light onto the city of Kapilavatthu. Suddenly the flag mounted on Indra's altar flapped violently and fell to the ground. Flowers of every color dropped like rain from the skies and the sound of celestial singing echoed everywhere throughout the capital. In her third dream, Yasodhara heard a loud voice that shook the heavens. "The time has come! The time has come!" it cried. Frightened, she looked over at Siddhartha's chair to discover he was gone. The jasmine flowers tucked in her hair fell to the floor and turned to dust. The garments and ornaments which Siddhartha had left on his chair transformed into a snake which slithered out the door. Yasodhara was filled with panic. All at once, she heard the bellowing of the white cow from beyond the city gates, the flapping of the flag upon Indra's altar, and the voices of heaven shouting, "The time has come! The time has come!"

Yasodhara awoke. Her forehead was drenched with sweat. She turned to Siddhartha and shook him. "Siddhartha, Siddhartha, please wake up."

He was already awake. He stroked her hair to comfort her and asked, "What did you dream, Gopa? Tell me."

She recounted all three dreams and then asked him, "Are these dreams an omen that you will soon leave me in order to go and seek the Way?"

Siddhartha fell silent, then consoled her, "Gopa, please don't worry. You are a woman of depth. You are my partner, the one who can help me to truly fulfill my quest. You understand me more than anyone else. If, in the near future, I must leave and travel far from you, I know you possess the courage to continue your work. You will care for and raise our child well. Though I am gone, though I am far away from you, my love for you remains the same. I will never stop loving you, Gopa. With that knowledge, you will be able to endure our separation. And when I have found the Way, I will return to you and to our child. Please, now try to get some rest."

Siddhartha's words, spoken so tenderly, penetrated Yasodhara's heart. Comforted, she closed her eyes and slept.

The following morning, Siddhartha went to speak to his father. "My royal father, I ask your permission to leave home and become a monk in order to seek the path of enlightenment."

King Suddhodana was greatly alarmed. Though he had long known this day might arrive, he had certainly not expected it to take place so abruptly. After a long moment, he looked at his son and answered, "In the history of our family, a few have become monks, but no one has ever done it at your age. They all waited until they were past fifty. Why can't you wait? Your son is still small, and the whole country is relying on you."

"Father, a day upon the throne would be like a day of sitting on a bed of hot coals for me. If my heart has no peace, how can I fulfill your or the people's trust in me? I have seen how quickly time passes, and I know my youth is no different. Please grant me your permission."

The king tried to dissuade his son. "You must think of your homeland, your parents, Yasodhara, and your son, who is still an infant."

"Father, it is precisely because I do think of all of you that I now ask your permission to go. It is not that I wish to abandon my responsibilities. Father, you know that you cannot free me from the suffering in my heart any more than you can release the suffering in your own heart."

The king stood up and grabbed his son's hand. "Siddhartha, you know how much I need you. You are the one on whom I have placed all my hopes. Please, don't abandon me."

"I will never abandon you. I am only asking you to let me go away for a time. When I have found the Way, I will return."

A look of pain crossed King Suddhodana's face. He said no more and retired to his quarters.

Later on, Queen Gotami came to spend the day with Yasodhara and in the early evening, Udayin, one of Siddhartha's friends, came to visit with Devadatta, Ananda, Bhadya, Anuruddha, Kimbila, and Bhadrika. Udayin had organized a party and had hired one of the finest dancing troupes in the capital to perform. Festive torches brightened the palace.

Gotami told Yasodhara that Udayin had been summoned by the king and given the task to do everything he could think of to entice Siddhartha to remain in the palace. The evening's party was the first of Udayin's plans.

Yasodhara instructed her attendants to prepare food and drinks for all the guests before retiring to her quarters with Gotami. Siddhartha himself went out and welcomed his guests. It was the full moon day of the month of Uttarasalha. As the music began, the moon appeared above a row of trees in the southeastern sky.

Gotami confided her thoughts to Yasodhara until it was late and then excused herself to return to her own residence. Yasodhara walked with her to the veranda where she saw the full moon now suspended high in the night sky. The party was still in full swing. Sounds of music, talking, and laughter drifted from within. Yasodhara led Gotami to the front gate and then went on her own to find Channa. He was already asleep when she found him. Yasodhara awoke him and whispered, "It is possible the prince will require your services tonight. Prepare Kanthaka to ride. And saddle another horse for yourself."

"Your highness, where is the prince going?"

"Please don't ask. Just do as I have said because the prince may need to ride tonight."

Channa nodded and entered the stable while Yasodhara returned inside the palace. She readied clothes suitable for traveling and placed them on Siddhartha's chair. She took a light blanket to cover Rahula and then lay upon the bed herself. As she lay there she listened to the sounds of music, talking, and laughter. It was a long time before the sounds faded, then disappeared. She knew the guests had retired to their quarters. Yasodhara lay quietly as silence returned to the palace. She waited a long time, but Siddhartha did not return to their room.

He was sitting alone outside, gazing at the radiant moon and stars. A thousand stars twinkled. He had made up his mind to leave the palace that very night. At long last, he entered his chamber and changed into the traveling clothes awaiting him there. He pulled back the curtain and gazed upon the bed. Gopa was lying there, no doubt asleep. Rahula was by her side. Siddhartha wanted to enter and speak words of parting to Yasodhara, but he hesitated. He had already said everything that was essential. If he woke her now, it would only make their parting more painful. He let the curtain drop and turned to leave. Again, he hesitated. Once more he lifted back the curtain to take a last look at his wife and son. He looked at them deeply as though to imprint on his memory that familiar and beloved scene. Then he released the curtain and walked out.

As he passed the guest hall, Siddhartha saw the slumbering dancing girls sprawled across the carpets. Their hair was undone and dishevelled; their mouths hung open like dead fish. Their arms, so soft and supple during the dance, now looked as stiff as boards. Their legs were tangled across each other's bodies like victims on a battlefield. Siddhartha felt as though he were crossing a cemetery.

He made his way to the stables and found Channa still awake.

"Channa, please saddle and bring Kanthaka to me."

Channa nodded. He had prepared everything. Kanthaka was already bridled and saddled. Channa asked, "May I accompany you, prince?"

Siddhartha nodded and Channa entered the stable for his own horse. They led the horses out of the palace grounds. Siddhartha stopped and stroked Kanthaka's mane. "Kanthaka," he spoke, "this is a most important night. You must give me your best for this journey."

He mounted Kanthaka and Channa mounted his horse. They walked them to avoid making any loud noise. The guards were fast asleep, and they passed through the city gates easily. Once well beyond the city gates, Siddhartha turned for a last look at the capital, now lying quietly beneath the moonlight. It was there that Siddhartha had been born and raised, the city where he had experienced so many joys and sorrows, so many anxieties and aspirations. In the same city now slept everyone close to him—his father, Gotami, Yasodhara, Rahula, and all the others. He whispered to himself, "If I do not find the Way, I will not return to Kapilavatthu."

He turned his horse toward the south and Kanthaka broke into a full gallop.

CHAPTER FIVE

Beginning Spiritual Practice

Even at a full gallop, they did not reach the border of Sakya until daybreak. Before them flowed the Anoma River, which they followed downstream until they found a shallow place to cross over with the horses. They rode for another spell before coming to the edge of a forest. A deer flitted in and out among the trees. Birds flew close by, undisturbed by the men's presence. Siddhartha dismounted. He smiled and stroked Kanthaka's mane.

"Kanthaka, you are wonderful. You have helped bring me here, and for that, I thank you."

The horse lifted his head and looked lovingly at his master. Siddhartha pulled out a sword tucked in his horse's saddle and then grasping his own long locks of hair in his left hand, cut them off with his right. Channa dismounted his own horse. Siddhartha handed him the hair and sword. He then removed his jeweled necklace.

"Channa, take my necklace, sword, and hair and give them to my father. Please tell him to have faith in me. I have not left home to selfishly avoid my responsibilities. I go now on behalf of all of you and all beings. Please, console the king and queen for me. Console Yasodhara. I ask this of you."

As Channa took the necklace, tears streamed from his eyes. "Your highness, everyone will suffer terribly. I don't know what I will say to the king and queen or to your wife, Yasodhara. Your highness, how will you sleep beneath the trees like an ascetic when all your life you've known nothing but a warm bed and soft blankets?"

Siddhartha smiled. "Don't worry, Channa. I can live the way others do. You must return to tell everyone of my decision before they begin to worry about my disappearance. Leave me here alone now."

Channa wiped his tears. "Please, your highness, let me stay here to serve you. Have mercy on me and don't make me bear such sorrowful news to ones I love!"

Siddhartha patted his attendant on the shoulder. His voice grew serious. "Channa, I need you to return and inform my family. If you truly care for me, please do as I say. I don't need you here, Channa. No monk has need of a personal attendant! Please, return home now!"

Channa reluctantly obeyed the prince. He carefully placed the hair and necklace inside his jacket and tucked the sword in Kanthaka's saddle. He grasped Siddhartha's arm in his two hands and beseeched him, "I will do as you say but please, your highness, remember me, and remember us all. Don't forget to return after you have found the Way."

Siddhartha nodded and smiled reassuringly at Channa. He stroked Kanthaka's head. "Kanthaka, my friend, now return home."

Channa held Kanthaka's reins and mounted his own steed. Kanthaka turned to look at Siddhartha one last time, his eyes filled with tears no less than Channa's.

Siddhartha waited until Channa and the two horses were out of sight before he turned toward the forest to enter his new life. The sky would now serve as his roof and the forest as his home. A sense of ease and contentment welled up within him. Just at that moment, a man came walking out of the forest. At first glance, Siddhartha thought he was a monk, for he was wearing the customary robe. But on closer inspection, Siddhartha saw the man was carrying a bow, and a quiver of arrows was slung across his back.

"You are a hunter, are you not?" asked Siddhartha.

"That is correct," the man answered.

"If you are a hunter, why are you dressed as a monk?"

The hunter smiled and said, "Thanks to this robe, the animals do not fear me, and I am thus easily able to shoot them."

Siddhartha shook his head. "Then you are abusing the compassion of those who follow a spiritual path. Would you agree to trade your robe for my garments?"

The hunter looked at Siddhartha and saw he was wearing royal garments of inestimable value.

"Do you really want to trade?" the hunter asked.

"Absolutely," said Siddhartha. "You could sell these garments and have enough money to stop hunting and begin a new trade. As for me, I wish to be a monk and have need of a robe like yours."

The hunter was overjoyed and, after exchanging his robe for Siddhartha's handsome clothes, he hurried off. Siddhartha now had the appearance of a real monk. He stepped into the forest and found a tree to sit beneath. For the first time as a homeless monk, he sat in meditation. After a long final day in the palace and an autumn night spent on the back of a horse, Siddhartha now experienced a marvelous ease. He sat in meditation to savor and nurture the feeling of release and freedom that had filled him the moment he entered the forest.

Sunlight filtered through the trees and came to rest on Siddhartha's eyelashes. He opened his eyes and saw standing before him, a monk. The monk's face and body were thin and worn by a life of austerities. Siddhartha stood up and joined his palms together in greeting. He told the monk he had only just abandoned his home and had not yet had the chance to be accepted by any teacher. He expressed his intent to travel south to find the spiritual center of Master Alara Kalama and there ask to be accepted as a disciple.

The monk told Siddhartha that he himself had studied under Master Alara Kalama and that at present the Master had started a center just north of the city Vesali. More than four hundred disciples were gathered there for his teaching.

The monk knew how to get there and said he would be glad to take Siddhartha.

Siddhartha followed him through the forest to a path which wound up a hill and entered another forest. They walked until noon, when the monk showed Siddhartha how to gather wild fruits and edible greens. The monk explained that it was sometimes necessary to dig roots to eat when there were no edible fruits or greens to be found. Siddhartha knew he would be living in the forests a long time and so he asked the names of all the edible foods and carefully noted everything the monk told him. He learned that the monk was an ascetic who lived on nothing but wild fruits, greens, and roots. His name was Bhargava. He told Siddhartha that Master Alara Kalama was not an ascetic and in addition to wild foraging, his monks begged for food or accepted what was brought as offerings to them from neighboring villages.

Nine days later, they reached the forest center of Alara Kalama, near Anupiya. They arrived as Master Alara was giving a talk to more than four hundred disciples. He looked about seventy years old and, though he appeared thin and frail, his eyes shone and his voice resounded like a copper drum. Siddhartha and his companion stood outside the circle of disciples and quietly listened to the Master's teaching. When he finished speaking, his disciples scattered throughout the forest to pursue their practice. Siddhartha approached him and after introducing himself, respectfully said, "Venerable Teacher, I ask you to accept me as one of your disciples. I wish to live and study under your guidance."

The master listened and looked intently at Siddhartha, and then expressed his approval. "Siddhartha, I would be happy to accept you. You may stay here. If you practice according to my teachings and methods, you will realize the teachings in a short time."

Siddhartha prostrated himself to express his happiness.

Master Alara lived in a straw hut made for him by several of his disciples. Scattered here and there in the forest were the straw huts of his followers. That night, Siddhartha found a level place to sleep, using a tree root for his pillow. Because he was exhausted from the long journey, he slept soundly until morning. When he awoke, the sun had already risen and the songs of birds filled the forest. He sat up.

The other monks had finished their morning meditation and were preparing to go down into the city to beg for food. Siddhartha was given a bowl and shown how to beg.

Following the other monks, he held his bowl and entered the city of Vesali. Holding a bowl to beg for the first time, Siddhartha was struck by how closely linked the life of a monk was to that of the laity—the monks were dependent on the lay community for food. He learned how to hold his bowl properly, how to walk and stand, how to receive the food offerings, and how to recite prayers in order to thank those who made the offerings. That day Siddhartha received some rice with curry sauce.

He returned with his new companions to the forest, and they all sat down to eat. When he had finished, he went to Master Alara to receive spiritual instruction. Alara was sitting in deep meditation when Siddhartha found him, and so he sat down before the master, quietly trying to focus his own mind. After a long time, Alara opened his eyes. Siddhartha prostrated himself and asked Master Alara to teach him.

Alara spoke to the new monk about faith and diligence and showed him how to use his breathing to develop concentration. He explained, "My teaching is not a mere theory. Knowledge is gained from direct experience and direct attainment, not from mental arguments. In order to attain different states of meditation, it is necessary to rid yourself of all thoughts of the past and future. You must focus on nothing but liberation."

Siddhartha asked about how to control the body and the sensations, and then respectfully thanked his teacher and walked away slowly to find a place in the forest where he could practice. He gathered branches and leaves and constructed a small hut beneath a sal tree where his meditation practice could ripen. He practiced diligently and, every five or six days, he returned to ask Alara's advice concerning whatever difficulties he was experiencing. In a short time, Siddhartha made considerable progress.

While sitting in meditation, he was able to let go of thoughts and even of clinging to his past and future, and he attained a state of wondrous serenity and rapture, although he felt the seeds of thought and attachment still present in him. Several weeks later, Siddhartha reached a higher state of meditation, and the seeds of thought and attachment dissolved. Then he entered a state of concentration in which both rapture and non-rapture ceased to exist. It felt to him as though the five doors of sense perception had completely closed, and his heart was as still as a lake on a windless day.

When he presented the fruits of his practice to Master Alara, the teacher was impressed. He told Siddhartha that he had made remarkable progress in a short time, and he taught Siddhartha how to realize the meditative state called the realm of limitless space, in which the mind becomes one with infinity, all material and visual phenomena cease to arise, and space is seen as the limitless source of all things.

Siddhartha followed his teacher's instructions and concentrated his efforts on achieving that state and in less than three days, he succeeded. But Siddhartha still felt that even the ability to experience infinite space had not liberated him from his deepest anxieties and sorrows. Dwelling in such a state of awareness, he still felt hindrances, so he returned to Alara for assistance. The master told him, "You must go one step further. The realm of limitless space is of the same essence as your own mind. It is not an object of your consciousness, but your very consciousness itself. Now you must experience the realm of limitless consciousness."

Siddhartha returned to his spot in the forest and in just two days, he realized the realm of limitless consciousness. He saw that his own mind was present in every phenomenon in the universe. But even with this attainment, he still felt oppressed by his deepest afflictions and anxieties. So Siddhartha returned to Master Alara and explained his difficulty. The master looked at him with eyes of deep respect and said, "You are very close to the final goal. Return to your hut and meditate on the illusory nature of all phenomena. Everything in the universe is created by our own minds. Our minds are the source of all phenomena. Form, sound, smell, taste, and tactile perceptions such as hot and cold, hard and soft—these are all creations of our minds. They do not exist as we usually think they do. Our consciousness is like an artist, painting every phenomenon into being. Once you have attained the state of the realm of no materiality, you will have succeeded. The realm of no materiality is the state in which we see that no phenomena exist outside of our own minds."

The young monk joined his palms to express his gratitude to his teacher, and returned to his corner of the forest.

While Siddhartha studied with Alara Kalama, he made the acquaintance of many other monks. Everyone was attracted by Siddhartha's kind and pleasant manner. Often, before Siddhartha had a chance to seek food for himself, he found food waiting for him by his hut. When he came out of meditation, he would find a few bananas or a rice ball secretly left for him by another monk. Many monks liked to befriend Siddhartha in order to learn from him, as they had heard their own master praise Siddhartha's progress.

Master Alara had once asked about Siddhartha's background and so learned of Siddhartha's life as a prince. But Siddhartha only smiled when other monks asked him about his royal past. He answered modestly, "It's nothing of importance. It would be best if we spoke only about our experiences of practicing the Way."

In less than a month, Siddhartha attained the state of the realm of no materiality. Happy to have achieved this state of awareness, he spent the following weeks trying to use it to dissolve the deepest obstructions in his mind and heart. But although the realm of no materiality was a profound state of meditation, it, too, was unable to help him. Finally, he returned to ask the advice of Master Alara Kalama.

Alara Kalama sat and listened intently to Siddhartha. His eyes shone. Expressing deepest respect and praise, he said, "Monk Siddhartha, you are profoundly gifted. You have attained the highest level I can teach. All I have attained, you have attained as well. Let us join together to guide and lead this community of monks."

Siddhartha was silent as he contemplated Alara's invitation. While the realm of no materiality was a precious fruit of meditation, it did not help resolve the fundamental problem of birth and death, nor did it liberate one from all suffering and anxiety. It did not lead to total liberation. Siddhartha's goal was not to become the leader of a community, but to find the path of true liberation.

Siddhartha joined his palms and answered, "Venerable Teacher, the state of the realm of no materiality is not the final goal I am seeking. Please accept my gratitude for your support and care, but now I must ask your permission to leave the community in order to seek the Way elsewhere. You have taught me with all your heart these past months and I will be forever grateful to you."

Master Alara Kalama looked disappointed, but Siddhartha had made up his mind. The next day, Siddhartha again took to the road.

CHAPTER SIX

Crossing the Ganga

Siddhartha crossed the Ganges River, known as the Ganga, and entered deep into the kingdom of Magadha, a region renowned for its accomplished spiritual teachers. He was determined to find someone who could teach him how to overcome birth and death. Most of the spiritual teachers lived in remote mountains or forests. Tirelessly, Siddhartha inquired about the whereabouts of these masters, and sought out each of them, no matter how many mountains and valleys he had to cross. He continued his search through rain and sun, from one month to the next.

Siddhartha met ascetics who refused to wear any clothes, and others who refused to accept any food offerings, living on only the fruits, greens, and roots that grew wild in the forests. Exposing their bodies to the elements, these ascetics believed that by enduring extreme austerities they would enter heaven after they died.

One day Siddhartha said to them, "Even if you are reborn in Heaven, the suffering on Earth will remain unchanged. To seek the Way is to find a solution to life's sufferings, not to escape life. Granted, we cannot accomplish much if we pamper our bodies like those who live for sensual pleasure, but abusing our bodies is no more helpful."

Siddhartha continued his search—remaining in some spiritual centers for three months and in others for six. His powers of meditation and concentration increased, but he was still unable to find the true path of liberation from birth and death. The months passed quickly, and soon it was more than three years since Siddhartha had left home. Sometimes, as he sat in meditation in the forests, images arose in Siddhartha's mind of his father, Yasodhara, and Rahula, and of his childhood and youth. Although it was difficult for him to avoid feeling impatient and discouraged, his strong faith that he would find the Way allowed him to continue his search.

During one period, Siddhartha dwelled alone on the hillside of Pandava, not far from the capital city of Rajagaha. One day he took his bowl and went down the hillside to beg in the capital. His walk was slow and dignified, his countenance serene and resolute. People on both sides of the street stopped to gaze at this monk who walked as elegantly as a lion passing through a mountain forest. The royal carriage of King Bimbisara of Magadha happened to pass by, and the king ordered his driver to stop so that he could have a good look at Siddhartha. He asked his attendant to offer the monk food and to follow him to see where he lived.

The next afternoon, King Bimbisara rode to Siddhartha's dwelling. Leaving his carriage at the foot of the hill, he mounted the path with one of his attendants. When he saw Siddhartha sitting beneath a tree, he approached to greet him.

Siddhartha stood up. He could tell by his visitor's dress that he was the king of Magadha. Siddhartha joined his palms together and then motioned for the king to sit on a large rock nearby. Siddhartha sat on another rock and faced the king.

King Bimbisara was noticeably impressed by the monk's noble bearing and elevated manner. He said, "I am the king of Magadha. I wish to invite you to come to the capital with me. I would like you by my side so that I may benefit from your teaching and virtue. With you at my side, I am sure the kingdom of Magadha would enjoy peace and prosperity."

Siddhartha smiled. "Great King, I am more used to living in the forest."

"This is too harsh a life. You have no bed, no attendant to assist you.

King Bimbisara was impressed by the monk's noble bearing and elevated manner.

If you agree to come with me, I will give you your own palace. Please return with me to teach."

"Great King, palace life is not well suited to me. I am endeavoring to find a path of liberation to free myself, and all beings, from suffering. Palace life is not compatible with the heart's quest of this monk."

"You are still young, as I am. I have need of a friend with whom I can truly share. From the moment I saw you, I felt a natural connection with you. Come with me. If you accept, I will reserve half of my kingdom for you and, when you are older, you can return to the life of a monk. It won't be too late."

"I thank you for your generous heart and offer of patronage, but I truly have but one desire, and that is to find the path that can liberate all beings from suffering. Time passes quickly. If I don't use the strength and energy I now possess as a young man, old age will arrive too soon, and I will feel deep regret. Life is so uncertain—sickness or death can occur at any moment. The flames of inner turmoil caused by greed, anger, hatred, passion, jealousy, and pride continue to burn in my heart. Only when the Great Way is discovered, will liberation be possible for all beings. If you truly feel affection for me, you will allow me to continue the path I have long pursued."

King Bimbisara was even more impressed after hearing Siddhartha speak. He said, "It gives me great joy to hear your words so filled with determination. Dear monk, allow me to ask where you are from and what your family name is."

"Great King, I come from the kingdom of Sakya. My family name is Sakya. King Suddhodana who presently rules in Kapilavatthu is my father, and my mother was Queen Mahamaya. I was the prince, heir to the throne, but because I wished to become a monk in order to seek the Way, I left my parents, wife, and son, more than three years ago."

King Bimbisara was astonished. "Then you yourself are of royal blood! I am most honored to meet you, noble monk! The royal families of Sakya and Magadha have long been on very close terms. How foolish of me to try to impress you with my position and wealth in order to persuade you to return with me. Please forgive me! Let me ask only this—from time to time, come to my palace and allow me to offer you food, and when you have found the Great Way, return in compassion to teach me as your disciple. Will you promise that?"

Siddhartha joined his palms and answered, "I promise that when I have discovered the path, I will return to share it with your highness."

King Bimbisara bowed low before Siddhartha and returned down the hill with his attendant.

Later that day, the monk Siddhartha Gautama abandoned his dwelling place to avoid the interruptions he feared would result from the young king bringing frequent offerings. Heading south, he looked for another place conducive to practice. He learned of the spiritual center of Uddaka Ramaputta, a great teacher who was said to have attained very deep levels of understanding. Three hundred monks were in residence at his center, located not far from Rajagaha, and four hundred other disciples practiced nearby. Siddhartha made his way there.

But as Siddhartha went to climb out of the water, his strength failed him.

CHAPTER SEVEN

Forest Ascetic

Master Uddaka was seventy-five years old. He was venerated by all as though he were a living god. Uddaka required all new disciples to begin at the most elementary levels of practice, so Siddhartha began again with the simplest meditation techniques. But in just a few weeks, he demonstrated to his new teacher that he had already attained the realm of no materiality, and Master Uddaka was impressed. He saw in this young man of noble bearing a potential spiritual heir, and he taught Siddhartha with utmost care.

"Monk Siddhartha Gautama, in the state of no materiality, emptiness is no longer the same as empty space, nor is it what is usually called consciousness. All that remains are perception and the object of perception. Thus, the path to liberation is to transcend all perception."

Siddhartha respectfully asked, "Master, if one eliminates perception, what is left? If there is no perception, how do we differ from a piece of wood or a rock?"

"A piece of wood or a rock is not without perception. Inanimate objects are themselves perception. You must arrive at a state of consciousness in which both perception and non-perception are eliminated. This is the state of neither perception nor non-perception. Young man, you must now attain that state."

Siddhartha left to return to his meditation. In just fifteen days, he realized the samadhi of neither perception nor non-perception.

Siddhartha saw that this state allowed one to transcend all ordinary states of consciousness. But whenever he came out of this meditative state, he saw that in spite of its extraordinariness, it did not provide a solution to the problem of life and death. It was a most peaceful state to dwell in, but it was not the key to unlock reality.

When Siddhartha returned to Master Uddaka Ramaputta, the Master praised him highly. He grasped Siddhartha's hand and said, "Monk Gautama, you are the best student I have ever had. You have made enormous progress in such a short time. You have attained the highest level I have. I am old and not long for this world. If you will remain here, we can guide this community together and when I die, you can take my place as Master of the community."

Once again, Siddhartha politely declined. He knew that the state of neither perception nor non-perception was not the key to liberation from birth and death, and that he had to move on. He expressed his deepest gratitude to the Master and to the community of monks, and took his leave. Everyone had come to love Siddhartha, and all were sad to see him go.

During his stay at Uddaka Ramaputta's center, Siddhartha made friends with a young monk named Kondanna. Kondanna was very fond of Siddhartha and regarded him as a teacher as well as a good friend. No one else in the community except Siddhartha had attained the state of no materiality, not to mention the state of neither perception nor non-perception. Kondanna knew that the Master considered Siddhartha worthy to be his spiritual heir. Just looking at Siddhartha gave Kondanna faith in his own practice. He often approached Siddhartha to learn from him, and a special bond grew between them. Kondanna regretted his friend's departure. He accompanied Siddhartha down the mountain and waited until he was no longer in sight before returning back up the mountain.

Siddhartha had accomplished so much with the masters reputed to be the two best meditation teachers in the land, and yet the fundamental issue of liberation from suffering was still burning inside him. He realized that he probably would not be able to learn much more from any of the other teacher-sages throughout the land, and so he knew that he had to seek the key to enlightenment on his own. Walking slowly west, between rice fields and across a long stretch of muddy lagoons and streams, Siddhartha reached the Neranjara River. He waded across it and walked until he reached Dangsiri Mountain, half a day's walk from Uruvela village. The steep and rocky slopes ended in saw-toothed peaks and concealed many caves. Boulders as large as the homes of poor villagers perched on the mountainside. Siddhartha resolved to remain here until he discovered the Way to Liberation. He found a cave in which he could sit in meditation for long hours and while sitting, he reviewed all the practices he had done for what was now more than five years. He remembered how he had advised the ascetics not to abuse their bodies, telling them that that would only add to the suffering of a world already filled with suffering. But now as he considered their path more carefully, he thought to himself, "You can't make a fire with soft, wet wood. The body is the same. If physical desires are not mastered, it is difficult for the heart to attain enlightenment. I will practice self-mortification in order to attain liberation."

Thus, the monk Gautama began a period of extreme asceticism. On dark nights, he entered the deepest and most wild reaches of the forest, the mere thought of which was enough to make a person's hair stand on end, and there he remained throughout the night. Even as fear and panic engulfed his mind and body, he sat without stirring. When a deer approached with its rustling sounds, his fear told him that these were demons coming to kill him, but he did not budge. When a peacock broke a piece of dead twig, his fear told him it was a python coming down from a tree, yet he still did not move, even as fear shot through him like the sting of red ants.

He tried to overcome all physical fears. He believed that once his body was no longer enslaved by fear, his mind would break the chains of suffering. Sometimes he sat with his teeth clenched while pressing his tongue against the roof of his mouth, using his willpower to suppress all fear and horror. Even when he broke into a cold sweat and his whole body became drenched, he did not move. At other times, he held his breath for long stretches until a roar like thunder or a blazing furnace pounded in his ears, and his head felt as though someone had taken an axe and cleaved it in two. Sometimes he felt as though his head was being squeezed by a steel band and his stomach slashed open like a goat's by a butcher. And at times, he felt as if his body was being roasted over an open fire. Through these austere practices, he was able to consolidate his courage and discipline, and his body was able to endure unspeakable pain, but his heart was still without peace.

The monk Gautama practiced austerities in this way for six months. For the first three of these months, he was alone on the mountain, but during the fourth month, he was discovered by five disciples of Master Uddaka Ramaputta, led by his old friend Kondanna. Siddhartha was happy to see Kondanna again, and he found out that just one month after Siddhartha left the meditation center, Kondanna himself had attained the state of neither perception nor non-perception. Seeing there was nothing more he could learn from Master Uddaka, Kondanna persuaded four friends to join him in seeking Siddhartha. After several weeks, they were lucky enough to find him, and they expressed their desire to stay and practice with him. Siddhartha explained to them why he was exploring the path of self-mortification, and the five young men, Kondanna, Vappa, Bhaddiya, Assaji, and Mahanama, resolved to join him. Each monk found a cave to live in, not far from one another, and every day one of them went into town to beg for food. When he returned, the food was divided into six portions so that none of them had more than a small handful each day.

Days and months went by, and the six monks grew thin and gaunt. They left the mountain and moved east toward the village of Uruvela, on the bank of the Neranjara, and continued to practice in the same way. But Siddhartha's austerities began to alarm even his five companions, and they found it impossible to keep up with him. Siddhartha ceased bathing in the river or even taking his share of the food. On some days he ate just a shrivelled guava he happened to find on the ground or a piece of dried buffalo manure. His body had become terribly wasted—it was little more than loose flesh hanging on protruding bones. He had not cut his hair or beard in six months, and when he rubbed his head, handfuls of hair fell out as though there was no longer any space for it to grow on the bit of flesh still clinging to his skull.

And then one day, while practicing sitting meditation in a cemetery, Siddhartha realized with a jolt how wrong the path of self-mortification was. The sun had set and a cool breeze gently caressed his skin. After sitting all day beneath the blazing sun, the breeze was delightfully refreshing, and Siddhartha experienced an ease in his mind unlike anything he had felt during the day. He realized that body and mind formed one reality, which could not be separated. The peace and comfort of the body were directly related to the peace and comfort of the mind. To abuse the body was to abuse the mind.

He remembered the first time he sat in meditation when he was nine years old, beneath the cool shade of a rose-apple tree on the day of the year's first plowing. He remembered how the refreshing ease of that sitting had brought him a sense of clarity and calm. He recalled, as well, his meditation in the forest right after Channa had left him. He thought back to his first days with Master Alara Kalama—those initial sessions of meditation had nourished both body and mind, creating in him a deep ability to concentrate and focus. But after that, Master Alara Kalama had told him to transcend the joys of meditation in order to attain states that existed beyond the material world, states such as the realms of limitless space and limitless consciousness, and the state of no materiality. Later, there had been the state of neither perception nor non-perception.

Always the goal had been to find a means to escape the world of feeling and thought, the world of sensation and perception. He asked himself, "Why follow only the traditions laid down in scripture? Why fear the joyful ease that meditation brings? Such joys have nothing in common with the five categories of desire which obscure awareness.

To the contrary, the joys of meditation can nourish body and mind, and provide the strength needed to pursue the path to enlightenment."

The monk Gautama resolved to regain his health and to use his meditation to nourish both body and mind. He would beg for food again starting the next morning. He would be his own teacher, not depending on the teachings of anyone else. Happy with this decision, he stretched out on a mound of earth and peacefully drifted off to sleep. The full moon had just risen in a cloudless sky, and the Milky Way stretched clear and radiant across the heavens.

The monk Gautama awoke the next morning to the sound of birds singing. He stood up and recalled his decisions of the previous night. He was covered with dirt and dust, and his robe was so tattered and threadbare it no longer covered his body. He remembered seeing a corpse in the cemetery the day before, and he guessed that today or tomorrow people would lift it down to the river to perform the cremation ceremony, and the brick-colored cloth that covered it would no longer be needed. He approached the corpse and, reflecting quietly on birth and death, respectfully removed the cloth from the body. The corpse was that of a young woman, her body swollen and discolored. Siddhartha would use the brick-colored cloth as a new robe.

He walked to the river to bathe himself and at the same time to wash the cloth. The water was cool, and Siddhartha found it overwhelmingly refreshing. He enjoyed the pleasant feeling of the water on his skin, welcoming the sensation with a new state of mind.

He took a long time bathing and then he scrubbed and wrung out his new robe. But as he went to climb out of the water, his strength failed him. He did not have enough energy to pull himself onto the bank. He stood quietly and breathed calmly. To one side he saw a tree branch leaning over the water, its leaves skimming the surface. He walked toward it slowly and grabbed on to it to support himself while he climbed out of the water.

He sat down to rest on the riverbank as the sun climbed higher into the sky. He spread out the cloth to dry in the hot sun and, when the cloth was dry, Siddhartha wrapped it around himself and set out for the village of Uruvela. But before he had walked even halfway, his strength failed him and, unable to catch his breath, he collapsed.

He lay unconscious for some time before a young girl from the village appeared. Thirteen-year-old Sujata had been sent by her mother to carry rice-milk, cakes, and lotus seeds to offer to the forest gods. When she saw the monk lying unconscious on the road, barely breathing, she knelt down and placed a bowl of milk to his lips. She knew he was an ascetic who had fainted from weakness.

When the drops of milk moistened his tongue and throat, Siddhartha responded immediately. He could taste how refreshing the milk was, and he slowly drank the entire bowlful. After a few dozen breaths, he was revived enough to sit up, and he motioned Sujata to pour him another bowlful of milk. It was remarkable how quickly the milk restored his strength. That day he decided to abandon austerity practice and go to the cool forest across the river to practice there.

During the days that followed, he gradually began to eat and drink normally. Sometimes Sujata brought him food offerings; sometimes he took his bowl into the village to beg. Every day he practiced walking meditation along the riverbank and the rest of the time he devoted to sitting meditation. Every evening he bathed in the Neranjara River. He abandoned all reliance on tradition and scripture in order to find the Way on his own. He returned to himself to learn from his own successes and failures. He did not hesitate to let meditation nourish his mind and body, and a sense of peace and ease grew within him. He did not distance himself or try to escape his feelings and perceptions, but maintained mindfulness in order to observe them as they arose.

He abandoned the desire to escape the world of phenomena and, as he returned to himself, he found he was completely present to the world of phenomena. One breath, one bird's song, one leaf, one ray of sunlight—any of these might serve as his subject of meditation. He began to see that the key to liberation lay in each breath, each step, each small pebble along the path.

The monk Gautama went from meditating on his body to meditating on his feelings, and from meditating on his feelings to meditating on his perceptions, including all the thoughts which rose and fell in his own mind. He saw the oneness of body and mind, that each and every cell of the body contained all the wisdom of the universe. He saw that he needed only to look deeply into a speck of dust to see the true face of the entire universe, that the speck of dust was itself the universe and, if it did not exist, the universe could not exist either. The monk Gautama went beyond the idea of a separate self, of *atman*, and, with a start, realized that he had long been dominated by a false view of atman as expounded in the Vedas. In reality, all things were without a separate self. Non-self, or *anatman*, was the nature of all existence. Anatman was not a term to describe some new entity. It was a thunderbolt that destroyed all wrong views. Taking hold of non-self, Siddhartha was like a general raising his sharp sword of insight on the battlefield of meditation practice. Day and night he sat beneath the pippala tree as new levels of awareness awoke in him like bright flashes of lightning.

During this time, Siddhartha's five friends lost faith in him. They saw him sitting along the riverbank eating food offerings. They watched him speak and smile to a young girl, enjoy milk and rice, and carry his bowl down into the village. Kondanna said to the others, "Siddhartha is no longer someone we can rely on. He has abandoned the path halfway. He now concerns himself only with idly feeding his body. We should leave him and seek another place to continue our practice. I see no reason to continue here."

Only after his five friends had departed, did Siddhartha notice their absence. Encouraged by his new insights, Siddhartha had devoted all his time to meditation and had not yet taken the time to explain this to his friends. He thought, "My friends have misunderstood me, but I can't worry now about convincing them otherwise. I must devote myself to finding the true path. Once I have found it, I will share it with them." Then he returned to his daily practice.

During those same days in which he made such great progress

along the path, the young buffalo boy Svasti appeared. Siddhartha cheerfully accepted the handfuls of fresh *kusa* grass the eleven-year-old boy offered for him to sit on. Though Sujata, Svasti, and their friends were still children, Siddhartha shared with them some of his new understanding. He was happy to see how unschooled children from the countryside could easily understand his discoveries. He was greatly heartened, for he knew that the door of complete enlightenment would soon open wide. He knew he held the wondrous key—the truth of the interdependent and non-self nature of all things.

Svasti brought Siddhartha a fresh armful of kusa grass.

CHAPTER EIGHT

Pippala Leaf

Beneath the pippala tree, the hermit Gautama focused all of his formidable powers of concentration to look deeply at his body. He saw that each cell of his body was like a drop of water in an endlessly flowing river of birth, existence, and death, and he could not find anything in the body that remained unchanged or that could be said to contain a separate self. Intermingled with the river of his body was the river of feelings in which every feeling was a drop of water. These drops also jostled with one another in a process of birth, existence, and death. Some feelings were pleasant, some unpleasant, and some neutral, but all of his feelings were impermanent: they appeared and disappeared just like the cells of his body.

With his great concentration, Gautama next explored the river of perceptions, which flowed alongside the rivers of body and feelings. The drops in the river of perceptions intermingled and influenced each other in their process of birth, existence, and death. If one's perceptions were accurate, reality revealed itself with ease; but if one's perceptions were erroneous, reality was veiled. People were caught in endless suffering because of their erroneous perceptions. They believed: that which is impermanent is permanent; that which is without self contains self; that which has no birth and death has birth and death; and they divided that which is inseparable into parts.

Gautama next shone his awareness on the mental states, which were the sources of suffering—fear, anger, hatred, arrogance, jealousy, greed, and ignorance. Mindful awareness blazed in him like a bright sun, and he used that sun of awareness to illuminate the nature of all these negative mental states. He saw that they all arose due to ignorance. They were the opposite of mindfulness. They were darkness—the absence of light. He saw that the key to liberation would be to break through ignorance and to enter deeply into the heart of reality and attain a direct experience of it. Such knowledge would not be the knowledge of the intellect, but of direct experience.

In the past, Siddhartha had looked for ways to vanquish fear, anger, and greed, but the methods he had used had not borne fruit because they were only attempts to suppress such feelings and emotions. Siddhartha now understood that their cause was ignorance, and that when one was liberated from ignorance, mental obstructions would vanish on their own, like shadows fleeing before the rising sun. Siddhartha's insight was the fruit of his deep concentration.

He smiled, and looked up at a pippala leaf imprinted against the blue sky, its tail blowing back and forth as if calling him. Looking deeply at the leaf, he saw clearly the presence of the sun and stars—without the sun, without light and warmth, the leaf could not exist. This was like this, because that was like that. He also saw in the leaf the presence of clouds—without clouds there could be no rain, and without rain the leaf could not be. He saw the earth, time, space, and mind—all were present in the leaf. In fact, at that very moment, the entire universe existed in that leaf. The reality of the leaf was a wondrous miracle.

Though we ordinarily think that a leaf is born in the springtime, Gautama could see that it had been there for a long, long time in the sunlight, the clouds, the tree, and in himself. Seeing that the leaf had never been born, he could see that he too had never been born. Both the leaf and he himself had simply manifested—they had never been born and were incapable of ever dying. With this insight, ideas of birth and death, appearance and disappearance dissolved, and the true face of the leaf and his own true face revealed themselves. He could see that the presence of any one phenomenon made possible the existence of all other phenomena. One included all, and all were contained in one. The leaf and his body were one. Neither possessed a separate, permanent self. Neither could exist independently from the rest of the universe. Seeing the interdependent nature of all phenomena, Siddhartha saw the empty nature of all phenomena—that all things are empty of a separate, isolated self. He realized that the key to liberation lay in these two principles of interdependence and non-self. Clouds drifted across the sky, forming a white background to the translucent pippala leaf. Perhaps that evening the clouds would encounter a cold front and transform into rain. Clouds were one manifestation; rain was another. Clouds also were not born and would not die. If the clouds understood that, Gautama thought, surely they would sing joyfully as they fell down as rain on to the mountains, forests, and rice fields.

Illuminating the rivers of his body, feelings, perceptions, mental formations, and consciousness, Siddhartha now understood that impermanence and emptiness of self are the very conditions necessary for life. Without impermanence and emptiness of self, nothing could grow or develop. If a grain of rice did not have the nature of impermanence and emptiness of self, it could not grow into a rice plant. If clouds were not empty of self and impermanent, they could not transform into rain. Without an impermanent, non-self nature, a child could never grow into an adult. "Thus," he thought, "to accept life means to accept impermanence and emptiness of self. The source of suffering is a false belief in permanence and the existence of separate selves. Seeing this, one understands that there is neither birth nor death; production nor destruction; one nor many; inner nor outer; large nor small; and impure nor pure. All such concepts are false distinctions created by the intellect. If one penetrates into the empty nature of all things, one will transcend all mental barriers, and be liberated from the cycle of suffering."

From one night to the next, Gautama meditated beneath the pippala tree, shining the light of his awareness on his body, his mind, and all the universe. His five companions had long abandoned him, and his co-practitioners were now the forest, the river, the birds, and the thousands of insects living on the earth and in the trees. The great pippala tree was his brother in practice. The evening star which appeared as he sat down in meditation each night was also his brother in practice. He meditated far into the night.

The village children came to visit him only in the early afternoons. One day Sujata brought him an offering of rice porridge cooked with milk and honey, and Svasti brought him a fresh armful of kusa grass to sit on. After Svasti left to lead the buffaloes home, Gautama was seized with a deep feeling that he would attain the Great Awakening that very night. Only the previous night he had had several unusual dreams. In one he saw himself lying on his side, his head pillowed by the Himalaya Mountains, his left hand touching the shores of the Eastern Sea, his right hand touching the shores of the Western Sea, and his two feet resting against the shores of the Southern Sea. In another dream, a great lotus as large as a carriage wheel grew from his navel and floated up to touch the highest clouds. In a third dream, birds of all colors, too many to be counted, flew towards him from all directions. These dreams seemed to announce that his Great Awakening was at hand.

Early that evening, Gautama did walking meditation along the banks of the river. He waded into the water and bathed. When twilight descended, he returned to sit beneath his familiar pippala tree. He smiled as he looked at the newly spread kusa grass at the foot of the tree. Beneath this very tree he had already made so many important discoveries in his meditation. Now the moment he had long awaited was approaching. The door to enlightenment was about to open.

Slowly, Siddhartha sat down in the lotus position. He looked at the river flowing quietly in the distance as soft breezes rustled the grasses along its banks. The night forest was tranquil yet very much alive. Around him chirped a thousand different insects. He turned his awareness to his breath and lightly closed his eyes. The evening star appeared in the sky.

CHAPTER NINE

The Morning Star Has Risen

Through mindfulness, Siddhartha's mind, body, and breath were perfectly at one. His practice of mindfulness had enabled him to build great powers of concentration, which he could now use to shine awareness on his mind and body. After deeply entering meditation, he began to discern the presence of countless other beings in his own body right in the present moment. Organic and inorganic beings, minerals, mosses and grasses, insects, animals, and people were all within him. He saw that other beings were himself right in the present moment. He saw his own past lives, all his births and deaths. He saw the creation and destruction of thousands of worlds and thousands of stars. He felt all the joys and sorrows of every living being—those born of mothers, those born of eggs, and those born of fission, who divided themselves into new creatures. He saw that every cell of his body contained all of Heaven and Earth, and spanned the three times—past, present, and future. It was the hour of the first watch of the night.

Gautama entered even more deeply into meditation. He saw how countless worlds arose and fell, were created and destroyed. He saw how countless beings pass through countless births and deaths. He saw that these births and deaths were but outward appearances and not true reality, just as millions of waves rise and fall incessantly on the surface of the sea, while the sea itself is beyond birth and death. If the waves understood that they themselves were water, they would

Svasti joined his palms and said, haltingly, "Teacher, you look so different today."

transcend birth and death and arrive at true inner peace, overcoming all fear. This realization enabled Gautama to transcend the net of birth and death, and he smiled. His smile was like a flower blossoming in the deep night which radiated a halo of light. It was the smile of a wondrous understanding, the insight into the destruction of all defilements. He attained this level of understanding by the second watch.

At just that moment thunder crashed, and great bolts of lightning flashed across the sky as if to rip the heavens in two. Black clouds concealed the moon and stars. Rain poured down. Gautama was soaking wet, but he did not budge. He continued his meditation.

Without wavering, he shined his awareness on his mind. He saw that living beings suffer because they do not understand that they share one common ground with all beings. Ignorance gives rise to a multitude of sorrows, confusions, and troubles. Greed, anger, arrogance, doubt, jealousy, and fear all have their roots in ignorance. When we learn to calm our minds in order to look deeply at the true nature of things, we can arrive at full understanding, which dissolves every sorrow and anxiety and gives rise to acceptance and love.

Gautama now saw that understanding and love are one. Without understanding, there can be no love. Each person's disposition is the result of physical, emotional, and social conditions. When we understand this, we cannot hate even a person who behaves cruelly, but we can strive to help transform his physical, emotional, and social conditions. Understanding gives rise to compassion and love, which in turn gives rise to correct action. In order to love, it is first necessary to understand, so understanding is the key to liberation. In order to attain clear understanding, it is necessary to live mindfully, making direct contact with life in the present moment, truly seeing what is taking place within and outside of oneself. Practicing mindfulness strengthens the ability to look deeply, and when we look deeply into the heart of anything, it will reveal itself. This is the secret treasure of mindfulness— it leads to the realization of liberation and enlightenment. Life is illuminated by right understanding, right thought, right speech, right action, right livelihood, right effort, right mindfulness, and right concentration. Siddhartha called this the Noble Path, *aryamarga*.

Looking deeply into the heart of all beings, Siddhartha attained insight into everyone's minds, no matter where they were, and he was able to hear everyone's cries of both suffering and joy. He attained the states of divine sight, divine hearing, and the ability to travel across all distances without moving. It was now the end of the third watch, and there was no more thunder. The clouds rolled back to reveal the bright moon and stars.

Gautama felt as though a prison, which had confined him for thousands of lifetimes, had broken open. Ignorance had been the jailkeeper. Because of ignorance, his mind had been obscured, just like the moon and stars hidden by the storm clouds. Clouded by endless waves of deluded thoughts, the mind had falsely divided reality into subject and object; self and others; existence and non-existence; and birth and death. From these discriminations arose wrong views—the prisons of feelings, craving, grasping, and becoming. The suffering of birth, old age, sickness, and death only made the prison walls thicker. The only thing to do was to seize the jailkeeper and see his true face. The jailkeeper was ignorance. And the way to overcome ignorance was the Noble Eightfold Path. Once the jailkeeper was gone, the jail would disappear and never be rebuilt again.

The hermit Gautama smiled, and whispered to himself, "O jailer, I see you now. How many lifetimes have you confined me in the prisons of birth and death? But now I see your face clearly, and from now on you can build no more prisons around me."

Looking up, Siddhartha saw the morning star appear on the horizon, twinkling like a huge diamond. He had seen this star so many times before while sitting beneath the pippala tree, but this morning it was like seeing it for the first time. It was as dazzling as the jubilant smile of enlightenment. Siddhartha gazed at the star and exclaimed out of deep compassion, "All beings contain within themselves the seeds of enlightenment, and yet we drown in the ocean of birth and death for so many thousands of lifetimes!"

Siddhartha knew he had found the Great Way. He had attained his goal, and now his heart experienced perfect peace and ease. He thought about his years of searching, filled with disappointments and hardships. He thought of his father, mother, aunt, Yasodhara, Rahula, and all his friends. He thought of the palace, Kapilavatthu, his people and country, and of all those who lived in hardship and poverty, especially children. He promised to find a way to share his discovery, to help all others liberate themselves from suffering. Out of his deep insight emerged a profound love for all beings.

Along the grassy riverbank, colorful flowers blossomed in the early morning sunlight. Sun danced on leaves and sparkled on the water. His pain was gone. All the wonders of life revealed themselves. Everything appeared strangely new. How wondrous were the blue skies and drifting white clouds! He felt as though he and all the universe had been newly created.

Just then, Svasti appeared. When Siddhartha saw the young buffalo boy come running toward him, he smiled. Suddenly Svasti stopped in his tracks and stared at Siddhartha, his mouth wide open. Siddhartha called, "Svasti!"

The boy came to his senses and answered, "Teacher!"

Svasti joined his palms and bowed. He took a few steps forward but then stopped and gazed again at Siddhartha in awe. Embarrassed by his own behavior, he spoke haltingly, "Teacher, you look so different today."

Siddhartha motioned for the boy to approach. He took him into his arms and asked, "How do I look different today?"

Gazing up at Siddhartha, Svasti answered, "It's hard to say. It's just that you look so different. It's like you are a star."

Siddhartha patted the boy on the head and said, "Is that so? What else do I look like?"

"You look like a lotus that's just blossomed. And like, like the moon over the Gayasisa Peak."

Siddhartha looked into Svasti's eyes and said, "Why, you're a poet,

Svasti! Now tell me, why are you here so early today? And where are your buffaloes?"

Svasti explained that he had the day off as all the buffaloes were being used to plow the fields. Only the calf had been left in its stall. Today his only responsibility was to cut grass. During the night he and his sisters and brother were awakened by the roar of thunder. Rain pounded through their leaky roof, soaking their beds. They had never experienced a storm so fierce, and they worried about Siddhartha in the forest. They huddled together until the storm subsided and they could fall back asleep. When day broke, Svasti ran to the buffaloes' stall to fetch his sickle and carrying pole, and made his way to the forest to see if Siddhartha was alright.

Siddhartha grasped Svasti's hand. "This is the happiest day I have ever known. If you can, bring all the children to come see me by the pippala tree this afternoon. Don't forget to bring your brother and sisters. But first go and cut the kusa grass you need for the buffaloes."

Svasti trotted off happily as Siddhartha began to take slow steps along the sun-bathed shore.

CHAPTER TEN

The Lotus Pond

Every day Siddhartha bathed in the Neranjara River. He did walking meditation along the riverbanks and along the small forest paths his own steps had created. He sat in meditation on the shore beside the flowing river or beneath the bodhi tree while hundreds of birds chirped among its branches. He had realized his vow. He knew he must return to Kapilavatthu where so many awaited news of his quest. He recalled, as well King Bimbisara in the city of Rajagaha. He felt a special affinity for the young king and wished to visit him. There were also his five former companions. He knew they each possessed the ability to attain liberation quickly, and he wanted to find them. No doubt they still dwelled nearby.

The children visited Siddhartha in the afternoons. He showed them how to sit still and to follow their breath in order to calm their minds when they felt sad or angry. He taught them walking meditation to refresh their minds and bodies. He taught them to look deeply at others and at their own actions in order to be able to see, to understand, and to love. The children understood all he taught them.

One day, after the children had returned home, Siddhartha did walking meditation. He lifted his robe to wade across the river, and then followed a path between two rice fields that led to a lotus pond he liked very much. There he sat down and contemplated the beautiful lotuses.

As he looked at the lotus stems, leaves, and flowers, he thought of all

It was the Buddha's custom to walk in meditation each morning along the riverbank.

the different stages of a lotus' growth. The roots remained buried in mud. Some stems had not risen above the surface of the water while others had barely emerged to reveal leaves still curled tightly shut. There were unopened lotus flower buds, those with petals just beginning to peek out, and lotus flowers in full bloom. There were seed pods from which all the petals had fallen. There were white lotus flowers, blue ones, and pink ones.

Siddhartha reflected that people were not very different from lotus flowers. Each person had his or her own natural disposition. Devadatta was not like Ananda; Yasodhara was not the same as Queen Pamita; Sujata was not like Bala, Svasti's sister. Personality, virtue, intelligence, and talent varied widely among people. The Path of Liberation which Siddhartha had discovered needed to be expounded in many ways to suit many kinds of people.

Different teaching methods were like gates by which different kinds of people could enter and understand the teaching. The creation of Dharma Gates would result from direct encounters with people. There were no ready-made methods miraculously received under the bodhi tree. Siddhartha saw that it would be necessary to return to society in order to set the wheel of Dharma in motion and to sow the seeds of liberation. Forty-nine days had passed since his Awakening. It was now time to depart from Uruvela. He decided to leave the following morning, parting from the cool forest by the banks of the Neranjara River, the bodhi tree, and the children. He wanted first to seek out his two teachers, Alara Kalama and Uddaka Ramaputta. He was confident that they would attain Awakening in no time at all. After assisting these two venerable men, he would find the five friends who had practiced austerities with him. Then he would return to Magadha to see King Bimbisara.

The next morning, Siddhartha put on a new robe the children had sewn for him and walked into Uruvela while the morning air was still misty. He went to Svasti's hut and told the young buffalo boy and his family that the time had come for him to depart. Siddhartha patted each of the children gently on the head, and together they walked to Sujata's house. Sujata cried when she learned the news.

Siddhartha said, "I must leave in order to fulfill my responsibilities. But I promise that I will return to visit you whenever I have a chance. You children have helped me very much and I am grateful. Please remember and practice the things I have shared with you. That way, I will never be far from you. Sujata, dry your tears now and give me a smile."

Sujata wiped her tears with the edge of her sari and tried to smile. Then the children walked with Siddhartha to the edge of the village. Siddhartha was turning to say farewell, when he noticed a young ascetic walking towards them. The ascetic joined his palms in greeting and looked curiously at Siddhartha. After a long moment, he said, "Monk, you look most radiant and peaceful. What is your name and who is your Master?"

Siddhartha answered, "My name is Siddhartha Gautama. I have studied with many teachers, but no one is my teacher now. What is your name, and where are you coming from?"

The ascetic answered, "My name is Upaka. I have just left the center of Master Uddaka Ramaputta."

"Is Master Uddaka in good health?"

"Master Uddaka died just a few days ago."

Siddhartha sighed. He would not have a chance to help his old teacher after all. He asked, "Have you ever studied with Master Alara Kalama?"

Upaka answered, "Yes. But he, too, has recently died."

"Do you by any chance know of a monk named Kondanna?"

Upaka said, "Yes, indeed. I heard about Kondanna and four other monks when I was living at Master Uddaka's center. I heard they are living and practicing together at the Deer Park in Isipatana, near the city of Varanasi. Gautama, if you will excuse me, I will continue on my way. I have a long day's journey ahead."

Siddhartha joined his palms to bid Upaka farewell, and then he turned to the children. "Children, I will follow the road to Varanasi to find my five friends. The sun has risen. Please return home now."

Siddhartha then followed the river northwards. He knew it would be a longer route but easier to travel. The Neranjara River led northwards to where it emptied into the Ganga. If he followed the westward course of the Ganga, he would reach the village of Pataligrama within a few days. There he could cross to the other side of the Ganga and reach Varanasi, the capital of Kasi.

The children gazed at him until he was out of sight. They were filled with terrible sadness and longing. They followed the riverbank back towards the village. No one spoke another word.

Kondanna took Siddhartha's begging bowl, Mahanama brought him water,
Bhaddiya pulled up a stool, and Vappa fanned him with a palm leaf,
while Assaji stood to one side, not knowing what to do.

CHAPTER ELEVEN

Turning the Wheel of Dharma

Assaji was practicing the austere way in the Deer Park. One day after his sitting meditation, he noticed a monk approaching from off in the distance. As the stranger came closer, he realized it was none other than Siddhartha, and he quickly told his four friends.

Bhaddiya said, "Siddhartha abandoned the path halfway. He ate rice, drank milk, and visited with the village children. He really let us down. I say we shouldn't even greet him." So the five friends agreed not to meet Siddhartha by the gate to the park. They also decided not to stand and greet him if he should enter the Deer Park by himself. But what actually took place was entirely different.

When Siddhartha entered the gate, the five ascetic companions were so impressed by his radiant bearing that they all stood up at once. Siddhartha seemed to be surrounded by an aura of light. Each step he took revealed a rare spiritual strength. His penetrating gaze undermined their intention to snub him. Kondanna ran up to him and took his begging bowl. Mahanama fetched water so that Siddhartha could wash his hands and feet. Bhaddiya pulled up a stool for him to sit on. Vappa found a fan of palm leaves and began to fan him. Assaji stood to one side, not knowing what to do.

After Siddhartha washed his hands and feet, Assaji realized he could fill a bowl with cool water and offer it to him. The five friends sat in a circle around Siddhartha, who looked kindly at them and said, "My brothers, I have found the Way, and I will show it to you."

Assaji half-believed and half-doubted Siddhartha's words. Perhaps the others felt the same, for no one spoke for a long moment. Then Kondanna blurted out, "Gautama! You abandoned the path halfway. You ate rice, drank milk, and spent time with the village children. How can you have found the path to liberation?"

Siddhartha looked into Kondanna's eyes and asked, "Friend Kondanna, you have known me a long time. During all that time, have I ever lied to you?"

Kondanna admitted that he had not. "Indeed, Siddhartha, I have never heard you speak anything but the truth."

Siddhartha said, "Then please listen, my friends. I have found the Great Way, and I will show it to you. You will be the first to hear my teaching. This Dharma is not the result of thinking. It is the fruit of direct experience. Listen serenely with all your awareness."

Siddhartha's voice was filled with such spiritual authority that his five friends joined their palms and looked up at him. Kondanna spoke for them all, "Please, friend Gautama, show us compassion and teach us the Way."

Siddhartha began serenely, "My brothers, there are two extremes that a person on the path should avoid. One is to plunge oneself into sensual pleasures, and the other is to practice austerities which deprive the body of its needs. Both of these extremes lead to failure. The path I have discovered is the Middle Way, which avoids both extremes and has the capacity to lead one to understanding, liberation, and peace. It is the Noble Eightfold Path of right understanding, right thought, right speech, right action, right livelihood, right effort, right mindfulness, and right concentration. I have followed this Noble Eightfold Path and have realized understanding, liberation, and peace.

"Brothers, why do I call this path the Right Path? I call it the Right Path because it does not avoid or deny suffering, but allows for a direct confrontation with suffering as the means to overcome it. The Noble Eightfold Path is the path of living in awareness. Mindfulness is the foundation. By practicing mindfulness, you can develop concentration, which enables you to attain understanding. Thanks to right concentration, you realize right awareness, thoughts, speech, action, livelihood, and effort. The understanding that develops can liberate you from every shackle of suffering and give birth to true peace and joy.

"Brothers, there are four truths: the existence of suffering, the cause of suffering, the cessation of suffering, and the path which leads to the cessation of suffering. I call these the Four Noble Truths. The first is the existence of suffering. Birth, old age, sickness, and death are suffering. Sadness, anger, jealousy, worry, anxiety, fear, and despair are suffering. Separation from loved ones is suffering. Association with those you hate is suffering. Desire, attachment, and clinging to the five aggregates are suffering.

"Brothers, the second truth reveals the cause of suffering. Because of ignorance, people cannot see the truth about life, and they become caught in the flames of desire, anger, jealousy, grief, worry, fear, and despair.

"Brothers, the third truth is the cessation of suffering. Understanding the truth of life brings about the cessation of every grief and sorrow, and gives rise to peace and joy.

"Brothers, the fourth truth is the path which leads to the cessation of suffering. It is the Noble Eightfold Path, which I have just explained. The Noble Eightfold Path is nourished by living mindfully. Mindfulness leads to concentration and understanding, which liberates you from every pain and sorrow, and leads to peace and joy. I will guide you along this path of realization."

While Siddhartha was explaining the Four Noble Truths, Kondanna suddenly felt a great light shining within his own heart. He could taste the liberation he had sought for so long. His face beamed with joy. The Buddha pointed at him and cried, "Kondanna! You've got it! You've got it!"

Kondanna joined his palms and bowed before Siddhartha. With deepest respect, he spoke, "Venerable Gautama, please accept me as your disciple. I know that under your guidance, I will attain the Great Awakening."

The other four monks also bowed at Siddhartha's feet, joined their palms, and asked to be received as disciples. Siddhartha motioned his friends to rise. After they took their places again, he said, "Brothers! The children of Uruvela village gave me the name 'the Buddha.' You, too, may call me by that name if you like."

Kondanna asked, "Doesn't 'Buddha' mean 'one who is awakened'?"

"That is correct. And they call the path I have discovered 'the Way of Awakening.' What do you think of this name?"

"'One who is awakened'! 'The Way of Awakening'! Wonderful! Wonderful! These names are true, yet simple. We will happily call you the Buddha and the path you have discovered the Way of Awakening. As you just said, living each day mindfully is the very basis of spiritual practice." The five monks were of one mind to accept Gautama as their teacher and to call him the Buddha.

The Buddha smiled at them. "Please, brothers, practice with an open and intelligent spirit, and in three months you will have attained the fruit of liberation."

The Buddha stayed in Isipatana to guide his five friends. Following his teaching, they gave up their practice of austerities. Every day three monks went begging for food and returned to share the offerings with the other three. The Buddha gave them individual attention, enabling each monk to make rapid progress.

The Buddha taught them about the impermanent and nonself nature of all things. He taught them to look at the five aggregates as five constantly flowing rivers which contained nothing that could be called separate or permanent. The five aggregates are the body, feelings, perceptions, mental formations, and consciousness. By meditating on the five aggregates within themselves, they came to see the intimate and wondrous connection between themselves and all in the universe.

Thanks to their diligence, they all realized the Way. The first to attain Awakening was Kondanna, followed two months later by Vappa and Bhaddiya. Shortly afterwards, Mahanama and Assaji also attained Arhatship, full enlightenment.

In great joy, the Buddha told them, "Now we have a real community, which we will call our sangha. The sangha is the community of those who live in harmony and awareness. We must take the seeds of awakening and sow them in all places.

*The Buddha liked to sit in meditation late into the night,
enjoying the moon and the cool air.*

CHAPTER TWELVE

Dharma Nectar

It was the Buddha's custom to rise early and to sit in meditation, and then do walking meditation among the forest trees. One morning while walking, he saw a handsome, elegantly dressed man in his late twenties, half-hidden in the morning mist. The Buddha sat on a large rock, and when the man approached quite close to the rock, still unaware of the Buddha, he mumbled, "Disgusting! Repulsive!"

The Buddha asked, "What is so disgusting? What is so repulsive?"

The young man introduced himself as Yasa, the son of one of the wealthiest and most reputable merchants in Varanasi. Yasa had always enjoyed a life of splendor and ease. His parents catered to his every whim, providing him with every kind of pleasure, including a handsome manor, jewels, money, wine, courtesans, banquets, and parties. But Yasa, a sensitive and thoughtful young man, had begun to feel suffocated by this life of pleasure and could no longer find any contentment in it.

He was like a person locked in a room without windows; he longed for some fresh air, for a simple, wholesome life. The night before, Yasa and some friends had gathered to feast, drink, play music, and be entertained by lovely young courtesans. In the middle of the night, Yasa woke up and looked at his friends and the young women sprawled out asleep. At that moment he knew he could not continue to live that way. He had wandered aimlessly all night until by chance he found himself in the Deer Park of Isipatana.

The Buddha counseled him, "Yasa, this life is filled with suffering, but it is also filled with many wonders. To drown in sensual pleasures is bad for the health of both the body and mind. If you live simply and wholesomely, not ruled by desires, it is possible to experience the many wonders of life. Yasa, look around you. Can you see the trees standing in the morning mists? Are they not beautiful? The moon, the stars, the rivers, the mountains, the sunlight, the songs of birds, and the sounds of bubbling springs are all manifestations of a universe that can provide us with endless happiness.

"The happiness we receive from these things nourishes the mind and body. Close your eyes, and breathe in and out a few times. Now open them. What do you see? Do you see trees, mist, sky, and rays of sunlight? Your own two eyes are wonders. Because you have been out of touch with wonders like these, you have come to despise your mind and body. Some people despise their own minds and bodies so much they want to commit suicide. They see only the suffering in life. But suffering is not the true nature of the universe. Suffering is the result of the way we live and of our erroneous understanding of life."

The Buddha's words touched Yasa like fresh drops of cool dew to soothe his parched heart. Overcome with happiness, he prostrated before the Buddha and asked to become a disciple.

The Buddha helped him up and said, "A monk lives a simple and humble life. He has no money. He sleeps in a grass hut or beneath the trees. He eats only what he receives from begging, and he eats only one meal a day. Can you live such a life?"

"Yes, Master, I would be happy to live such a life."

The Buddha continued, "A monk devotes his mind and body to realizing liberation, in order to help himself and all others. He concentrates his efforts to help relieve suffering. Do you vow to follow such a path?"

"Yes, Master, I vow to follow such a path."

"Then I accept you as my disciple. A disciple in my community is known as a *bhikkhu*, a beggar. Every day you will go to beg for your food in order to nourish yourself, to practice humility, and to be in touch with others in order to show them the Way."

News of Yasa becoming a bhikkhu spread quickly among his friends. His closest companions—Vimala, Subahu, Punnaji, and Gavampati—decided to visit him at Isipatana. On the way there Subahu said, "If Yasa has decided to become a monk, his Master must really be extraordinary and the path he teaches most lofty. Yasa is very discriminating."

Vimala retorted, "Don't be so certain. Perhaps he became a monk on a whim, and it won't last long. After six months or a year, he may very well abandon such a life."

Gavampati disagreed. "You're not taking Yasa seriously enough. I have always found him to be quite serious, and I'm sure he wouldn't do anything like this without sincerely intending it."

When they found Yasa at the Deer Park, he introduced them to the Buddha. "Teacher, these four friends of mine are all fine persons. Please have compassion and open their eyes to the path of liberation."

The Buddha sat down to talk with the four young men. At first Vimala was the most skeptical, but the more he heard the more impressed he became. Finally, he suggested to the other three that they all ask the Buddha to accept them as bhikkhus. The four young men knelt before the Buddha. Recognizing their sincerity, the Buddha accepted them on the spot. He asked Kondanna to give them basic instruction.

Yasa had several hundred other friends who soon heard how Yasa and his four closest companions had all become bhikkhus. One hundred and twenty of these young men decided to visit Isipatana that very morning. Yasa was informed of their arrival and he came out to greet them. He spoke about his decision to become a bhikkhu and then he led them to have an audience with the Buddha.

Surrounded by the young men, the Buddha spoke about the path which can end suffering and lead to peace and joy. He told them about his own search and how he had vowed to find the Way while he was still a young man. The one hundred and twenty young men listened as if entranced. Fifty of them requested to become bhikkhus at once.

Many of the other seventy also wanted to become bhikkhus but could not abandon their responsibilities as sons, husbands, and fathers. Yasa asked the Buddha to accept his fifty friends, and the Buddha agreed.

The Buddha now had sixty bhikkhus living with him at the Deer Park. He remained there for three additional months in order to guide the community. During that time, the Buddha accepted several hundred men and women as lay disciples.

Before long, many people in the kingdoms of Kasi and Magadha heard about the Buddha and his disciples. They knew that a prince of the Sakya clan had attained liberation and was teaching his path in Isipatana, near the city of Varanasi. Many monks who, up to then, had not yet attained the fruits of liberation, felt greatly encouraged, and they came from all directions to Isipatana. After hearing the Buddha speak, most took vows to become bhikkhus. The bhikkhus who had left Isipatana to spread the teaching brought back many more young men who also wished to become monks. The number of disciples soon swelled.

One day the Buddha gathered the sangha in the Deer Park and said, "Bhikkhus! It is no longer necessary for me personally to ordain every new bhikkhu or for everyone who wishes to be ordained to come to Isipatana. Those who wish to receive ordination should be able to do so in their own villages, in the presence of their friends and families. And, like you, I too would like to be free to remain here and to travel from here. Henceforth, when you meet a sincere and aspiring new bhikkhu, you may ordain him wherever you may be."

Kondanna stood up and joined his palms. "Master, please show us the way to organize a ceremony of ordination. Then we can do it by ourselves in the future."

The Buddha answered, "Please do as I have done in the past."

Assaji stood up and said, "Master, your presence is so formidable, you do not need to perform a formal ceremony. But for the rest of us, a formal procedure is needed. Brother Kondanna, perhaps you can suggest a form. The Buddha is here with us and he can add to your suggestions."

Kondanna was silent for a moment. Then he spoke, "Respected Buddha,

I think the first step should be to have the aspiring bhikkhu allow his hair and beard to be shaved. Then he can be instructed in the manner of wearing the robe. After he has put on his robe, he can expose his right shoulder in the customary manner and kneel before the monk giving the ordination. It is proper to kneel as the monk giving the ordination is serving as the representative of the Buddha. The one being ordained can hold his palms together like a lotus bud and recite three times, 'I take refuge in the Buddha, the one who shows me the way in this life. I take refuge in the Dharma, the way of understanding and love. I take refuge in the Sangha, the community that lives in harmony and awareness.' After repeating these refuges, he will be considered a bhikkhu in the community of the Buddha. But this is only my poor suggestion. Please, Teacher, correct it."

The Buddha answered, "It is most fine, Brother Kondanna. Reciting the three refuges three times while kneeling before an already ordained bhikkhu shall be sufficient to become an ordained bhikkhu." The community was happy with this decision.

A few days later the Buddha put on his robe, lifted his bowl, and left Isipatana on his own. It was an especially beautiful morning. He headed towards the Ganga River to return to Magadha.

The Buddha had traveled the road from Varanasi to Rajagaha before. He walked slowly and enjoyed the surrounding forests and rice fields. He crossed the Ganga and headed east. He wanted to visit the children of Uruvela before making his way to Rajagaha to see King Bimbisara.

Seven days later, the Buddha was happy to find himself back in the forest of the bodhi tree. The village children came to visit the Buddha in the forest. They were very happy to see the Buddha again and listened intently while he told them all that had happened to him in the past year.

The children told the Buddha that over the past few months a spiritual community led by a brahman had settled nearby. There were five hundred devotees in all. They worshipped the God of Fire. The brahman's name was Kassapa. He was deeply revered by all who met him.

The following morning, the Buddha crossed the river and found Master Kassapa's community. His devotees lived in simple huts made from leafy branches and wore clothes made from the bark of trees. They did not enter the village to beg but accepted offerings brought to them by the villagers. The Buddha stopped to speak with one of Kassapa's followers who told him that Kassapa was deeply versed in the Vedas and lived a life of utmost virtue. Kassapa, he explained, also had two younger brothers who also led communities of fire worship. All three brothers held fire to be the original essence of the universe. Uruvela Kassapa was deeply loved by his two brothers—Nadi Kassapa, who lived with three hundred devotees along the Neranjara about a day's travel north, and Gaya Kassapa who led two hundred devotees in Gaya.

Kassapa's disciple led the Buddha to his master's hut so that the Buddha could have an audience with him. Although Kassapa was no longer a young man, he was still quick and alert. When he saw the young teacher's extraordinary bearing, he felt immediately drawn to him and treated him as a special guest. Kassapa invited the Buddha to sit on a stump outside the hut, and the two enjoyed a long conversation. Kassapa marveled at how deeply versed the Buddha was in the Vedas. He was further astounded to discover that this young monk had grasped certain concepts in the Vedas that had eluded his own understanding. The Buddha helped explain certain of the most profound passages in the Atharveda and Rigveda scriptures, which Kassapa thought he had understood but discovered he had not yet truly grasped. Even more amazing was the young monk's knowledge of history, doctrine, and brahmanic rituals.

That noon the Buddha accepted Uruvela Kassapa's invitation to have a meal with him. The Buddha neatly folded his outer robe into a cushion and sat upon it, eating in mindful silence. So impressed was Uruvela Kassapa by the Buddha's serene and majestic countenance that he did not break the silence.

That afternoon they continued their conversation. The Buddha asked, "Master Kassapa, can you explain to me how worshipping fire can lead a person to liberation?"

Uruvela Kassapa did not answer right away. He knew very well that a superficial or ordinary response would not suffice for this extraordinary young monk. Kassapa began by explaining that fire was the basic essence of the universe. It had its source in Brahma. The main altar of the community, the Fire Sanctuary, always kept a sacred fire burning. That fire was itself the image of Brahma. The Atharveda scripture spoke of fire worship. Fire was life. Without fire there could be no life. Fire was light, warmth, and the source of the sun, which enabled plants, animals, and people to live. It chased away dark shadows, conquered the cold, and brought joy and vitality to all beings. Food was made edible by fire, and thanks to fire, people were reunited with Brahma at death. Because fire was the source of life, it was Brahma himself. Agni, the god of fire, was one of the thousands of manifestations of Brahma. A devotee in their community had to observe precepts, practice austerities, and pray diligently in order to follow the path that would one day lead to liberation.

Kassapa was strongly opposed to those brahmans who used their position in society to acquire wealth and lose themselves in pursuit of sensual pleasures. He said that such brahmans only performed rituals and recited the scriptures in order to become rich. Because of that, the reputation of the traditional brahmanic path had become tarnished.

The Buddha asked, "Master Kassapa, what do you think of those who regard water as the fundamental essence of life, who say that water is the element which purifies and returns people to union with Brahma?" Kassapa hesitated. He thought of the hundreds of thousands of people, right at that very moment, who were bathing themselves in the waters of the Ganga and other sacred rivers to purify themselves.

"Gautama, water cannot really help one attain liberation. Water naturally flows down. Only fire rises. When we die, our body rises in smoke thanks to fire."

"Master Kassapa, that is not accurate. The white clouds floating above are also a form of water. Thus, water rises too. Indeed, smoke itself is no more than evaporated water. Both clouds and smoke will eventually return to a liquid state. All things, as I'm sure you know, move in cycles."

"But all things share one fundamental essence and all things return to that one essence."

"Master Kassapa, all things depend on all other things for their existence. Take, for example, this leaf in my hand. Earth, water, heat, seed, tree, clouds, sun, time, and space—all these elements have enabled this leaf to come into existence. If just one of these elements was missing, the leaf could not exist. All beings, organic and inorganic, rely on the law of dependent co-arising. The source of one thing is all things. Please consider this carefully. Don't you see that this leaf I am now holding in my hand is only here thanks to the interpenetration of all the phenomena in the universe, including your own awareness?"

It was already evening and beginning to grow dark. Kassapa invited the Buddha to sleep in his own hut. It was the first time he had ever made such an offer to anyone, but then he had never before met such an extraordinary monk. But the Buddha refused, saying that he had grown accustomed to sleeping alone at night. He said he would like to sleep in the Fire Sanctuary if that would be all right.

The next day they sat by the lotus pond and conversed. Kassapa said, "Yesterday you said that the presence of a leaf resulted from the coming together of many different conditions. You said that humans, too, exist only because of the coming together of many other conditions. But when all these conditions cease to be, where does the self go?"

The Buddha answered, "For a long time humans have been trapped by the concept of atman, the concept of a separate and eternal self. We have believed that when our body dies, this self continues to exist and seeks union with its source, which is Brahma. But, friend Kassapa, that is a fundamental misunderstanding, which has caused countless generations to go astray.

"You should know, friend Kassapa, that all things exist because of interdependence and all things cease to be because of interdependence. This is because that is. This is not because that is not. This is born because that is born. This dies because that dies. This is the wonderful law of dependent co-arising which I have discovered in my meditation. In truth, there is nothing which is separate and eternal. There is no self, whether a higher or a lower self. Kassapa, have you ever meditated on your body, feelings, perceptions, mental formations, and consciousness? A person is made up of these five aggregates. They are continuously changing rivers in which one cannot find even one permanent element."

Uruvela Kassapa remained silent for a long moment. Then he asked, "Could one say then that you teach the doctrine of non-being?"

The Buddha smiled and shook his head. "No. The concept of non-being is one narrow view among a whole forest of narrow views. The concept of non-being is just as false as the concept of a separate, permanent self. Kassapa, look at the surface of this lotus pond. I do not say that the water and lotus do not exist. I only say that the water and the lotus arise thanks to the presence and interpenetration of all other elements, none of which are separate or permanent."

Kassapa lifted his head and looked into the Buddha's eyes. "If there is no self, no atman, why should one practice a spiritual path in order to attain liberation? Who will be liberated?"

The Buddha looked deeply into the eyes of his brahmana friend. His gaze was as radiant as the sun and as gentle as the soft moonlight. He smiled and said, "Kassapa, look for the answer within yourself."

They returned together to Kassapa's community. Uruvela Kassapa insisted on giving the Buddha his hut for the night, and went to sleep himself in the hut of one of his senior disciples. The Buddha could see how deeply Kassapa's disciples revered their teacher.

One afternoon, while the Buddha and Kassapa stood along the banks of the Neranjara, Kassapa said, "Gautama, the other day you spoke about the meditation on one's body, feelings, perceptions, mental formations, and consciousness. I have been practicing that meditation and I have begun to understand how one's feelings and perceptions determine the quality of one's life. I also see that there is no permanent element to be found in any of the five rivers. I can even see that the belief in a separate self is false. But I still don't understand why one should follow a spiritual path if there is no self? Who is there to be liberated?"

The Buddha asked, "Kassapa, do you accept that suffering is a truth?"

"Yes, Gautama, I accept that suffering is a truth."

"Do you agree that suffering has causes?"

"Yes, I accept that suffering has causes."

"Kassapa, when the causes of suffering are present, suffering is present. When the causes of suffering are removed, suffering is also removed."

"Yes, I see that when the causes of suffering are removed, suffering itself is removed."

"The cause of suffering is ignorance, a false way of looking at reality. Thinking the impermanent is permanent, that is ignorance. Thinking there is a self when there is not, that is ignorance. From ignorance is born greed, anger, fear, jealousy, and countless other sufferings. The path of liberation is the path of looking deeply at things in order to truly realize the nature of impermanence, the absence of a separate self, and the interdependence of all things. This path is the path which overcomes ignorance. Once ignorance is overcome, suffering is transcended. That is true liberation. There is no need for a self for there to be liberation."

Uruvela Kassapa sat silently for a moment and then said, "Gautama, I know you speak only from your own direct experience. Your words do not simply express concepts. You have said that liberation can only be attained through the efforts of meditation, by looking deeply at things. Do you think that all ceremonies, rituals, and prayers are useless?"

The Buddha pointed to the other side of the river and said, "Kassapa, if a person wants to cross to the other shore, what should he do?"

"If the water is shallow enough, he can wade across. Otherwise he will have to swim or row a boat across."

"I agree. But what if he is unwilling to wade, swim, or row a boat? What if he just stands on this side of the river and prays to the other shore to come to him? What would you think of such a man?"

"I would say he was being quite foolish!"

"Just so, Kassapa! If one doesn't overcome ignorance and mental obstructions, one cannot cross to the other side to liberation, even if one spends one's whole life praying."

Suddenly Kassapa burst into tears and prostrated himself before the Buddha's feet. "Gautama, I have wasted more than half my life. Please accept me as your disciple and give me the chance to study and practice the way of liberation with you."

The Buddha helped Kassapa stand back up and said, "I would not hesitate to accept you as my disciple, but what of your five hundred devotees? Who will guide them if you leave?"

Kassapa answered, "Gautama, give me a chance to speak with them this morning. Tomorrow afternoon I will let you know of my decision."

The Buddha said, "The children in Uruvela village call me the Buddha."

Kassapa was surprised. "That means the Awakened One, doesn't it? I will call you the same."

The next morning, the Buddha went begging in Uruvela village. Afterward he went to the lotus pond to sit. Late that afternoon, Kassapa came looking for him. He told the Buddha that all five hundred of his devotees agreed to become disciples under the Buddha's guidance.

The next day, Uruvela Kassapa and all his followers shaved their heads and beards, and threw the locks of hair into the Neranjara River along with all the liturgical objects they had used for fire worship. They bowed before the Buddha and recited three times, "I take refuge in the Buddha, the one who shows me the way in this life. I take refuge in the Dharma, the way of understanding and love. I take refuge in the Sangha, the community that lives in harmony and awareness." Their recitation of the three refuges echoed throughout the forest.

When the ordination was completed, the Buddha spoke to the new bhikkhus about the Four Noble Truths and how to observe one's breath, body, and mind. He showed them how to beg for food and how to eat in silence. He asked them to release all the animals they had once raised for food and sacrifices.

The next day Nadi Kassapa, Uruvela Kassapa's younger brother, arrived. Uruvela Kassapa returned from begging with the Buddha and was most happy to see his younger brother. He invited him for a walk in the forest. They were gone for a good length of time, and when they returned Nadi Kassapa announced that he and his three hundred devotees would also take refuge in the Buddha. Both brothers agreed to send someone to summon their brother, Gaya Kassapa. Thus, in the space of only seven days, the two hundred devotees of Gaya Kassapa were also ordained as bhikkhus. The Kassapa brothers were well known for their brotherly love and sharing of common ideals. Together they became deeply devoted students of the Buddha.

The Buddha remained in Gayasisa for three months to teach the new bhikkhus, and the bhikkhus made great progress. The Kassapa brothers were talented assistants to the Buddha, and they helped him guide and teach the sangha.

The morning had arrived for the Buddha to depart from Gayasisa and make his way to Rajagaha. He traveled in the company of all nine hundred bhikkhus. When they neared Rajagaha, Uruvela Kassapa led them to Palm Forest where the Supatthita Temple was located.

By the end of two weeks, most of the city was aware of the presence of the Buddha's sangha. On cool afternoons, many laypersons came to Palm Forest to meet the Buddha and to learn about the Way of Awakening. Before the Buddha had had a chance to visit his friend, the young King Bimbisara had already learned of the Buddha's presence. Sure that this new teacher was the same young monk he had met on the mountain, he mounted his carriage and ordered it driven to Palm Forest. Many other carriages followed his, for he had invited over a hundred highly regarded brahmana teachers and intellectuals to join him. When they reached the edge of the forest, the king stepped out of his carriage, accompanied by the queen and their son, Prince Ajatasattu. Among the guests were many scholars well-versed in the Vedas and belonging to many different schools of religious thought.

The Buddha spoke about the Way of Awakening. He spoke about the impermanent and interdependent nature of all things in life. He said that the Path of Awakening could help one overcome false views and transcend suffering. He spoke about how observing the precepts could help one attain concentration and understanding. His voice resounded like a great bell. It was as warm as spring sunshine, as gentle as a light rain, and as majestic as the rising tide. More than one thousand people listened. No one dared to breathe too loudly or rustle their robes for fear of disturbing the sound of the Buddha's wondrous voice.

King Bimbisara's eyes grew brighter by the moment. The more he listened, the more he felt his heart open. So many of his doubts and troubles vanished. A radiant smile appeared on his face. When the Buddha concluded his Dharma talk, King Bimbisara stood up and joined his palms. He said, "Lord, from the time I was young, I had five wishes. I have now fulfilled them all. The first wish was to receive coronation and become king; that has been fulfilled. The second wish was to meet in this very life an enlightened teacher; that has also been fulfilled. The third wish was to have a chance to show respect to such a teacher; that wish has now been fulfilled. The fourth wish was to have such a teacher show me the true path; that wish has now been fulfilled. And the fifth wish was to be able to understand the teaching of the Enlightened One; Master, this wish has just been fulfilled. Your wondrous teaching has brought me much understanding. Lord, please accept me as your lay disciple." The Buddha smiled his acceptance.

The king invited the Buddha and all nine hundred of his bhikkhus to have a meal at the palace on the day of the full moon. The Buddha gladly accepted.

All the other guests stood up to thank the Buddha. Twenty of them expressed the desire to be accepted as the Buddha's disciples. The Buddha and Uruvela Kassapa accompanied the king, queen, and little Prince Ajatasattu back to the edge of the forest.

The Buddha knew that in less than a month, the rainy season would begin, and it would be impossible to return to his homeland. Therefore, he resolved to remain with the nine hundred bhikkhus in Palm Forest for another three months. He knew that after three months of practice, the sangha would be strong and stable enough for him to depart. He would leave in the spring, the season of clear skies and tender new plants.

Throughout the following weeks, many seekers—many of them highly-educated young men—came to the Buddha and asked to be ordained as bhikkhus. The Buddha's senior students performed the ordination ceremonies and gave the new bhikkhus basic instruction in the practice. Other young people, women as well as men, came to Palm Forest and took the three refuges to become lay disciples of the Buddha.

During those same days, the Buddha received two exceptional new disciples, Sariputta and Moggallana, into his sangha of bhikkhus. They were both disciples of the famous ascetic Sanjaya, who lived in Rajagaha. Sanjaya's devotees were called *parivrajakas*. Sariputta and Moggallana were close friends, respected for their intelligence and open-mindedness. They had promised each other that whoever attained the Great Way first would immediately inform the other.

One day Sariputta saw the bhikkhu Assaji begging in Rajagaha, and he was immediately drawn by Assaji's relaxed and serene bearing. Sariputta thought to himself, "This appears to be someone who has attained the Way. I knew such persons could be found! I will ask him who his teacher is and what his teaching is."

Sariputta quickened his pace to catch up with Assaji but then stopped himself, not wanting to disturb the bhikkhu while he was silently begging from house to house. Sariputta resolved to wait until Assaji was finished begging before approaching him. Without making himself noticed, Sariputta followed Assaji. When Assaji's bowl was filled with offerings and he turned to leave the city, Sariputta joined his palms in respectful greeting and said, "Monk, you radiate such peace and calm. Your virtue and understanding shine in the way you walk, in the expression on your face, and in your every gesture. Please allow me to ask who your teacher is and at what practice center you reside. What methods does your teacher teach?"

Assaji looked at Sariputta for a moment and then smiled in a most friendly manner. He answered, "I study and practice under the guidance of the Master Gautama of the Sakya clan who is known as the Buddha. He is presently dwelling near Supatthita Temple in Palm Forest."

Sariputta's eyes brightened. "What is his teaching? Can you share it with me?"

"The Buddha's teaching is deep and lovely. I have not grasped it fully yet. You should come and receive the teachings directly from the Buddha."

But Sariputta implored Assaji, "Please, can't you share with me even a few words of the Buddha's teaching? It would be so precious to me. I will come for more teaching later."

Assaji smiled and then recited a short *gatha*:

> From interdependent origins
> all things arise
> and all things pass away.
> So teaches the
> Perfectly Enlightened One.

Sariputta suddenly felt his heart open as though it were being flooded by bright light. A flawless glimpse of true Dharma flashed before him. He bowed to Assaji and quickly ran to seek his friend Moggallana.

When Moggallana saw Sariputta's radiant face, he asked, "My brother, what has made you so happy? Can you have found the true path? Please tell me, brother!"

Sariputta related what had just happened. When he recited the gatha for Moggallana to hear, Moggallana also felt a sudden flash of light illuminate his heart and mind. Suddenly he saw the universe as an interconnected net. This was because that was; this arose because that arose; this was not because that was not; this passed away because that passed away. The belief in a creator of all things vanished in this understanding of dependent co-arising. He now understood how one could cut through the endless cycle of birth and death. The door of liberation opened before him.

Moggallana said, "Brother, we must go to the Buddha at once. He is the teacher we have been waiting for."

Sariputta agreed, but reminded him, "What of the two hundred fifty parivrajaka brothers who have long placed their faith and trust in us as elder brothers of the community? We can't just abandon them. We must go and inform them of our decision first."

The two friends made their way to the parivrajaka main gathering place and explained to their fellow practitioners their decision to leave the community and become disciples of the Buddha. When the parivrajakas heard that Sariputta and Moggallana were about to leave them, they were grieved. The community would not be the same without these two elder brothers. And so, they all expressed their desire to follow them and become disciples of the Buddha, too.

Sariputta and Moggallana went to Master Sanjaya and told him of the decision of the community. He entreated them to stay, saying "If you remain here, I will transfer the leadership of the community to you both." He said this three times, but Sariputta and Moggallana had made up their minds.

They said, "Respected Master, we embarked on the spiritual path in order to find liberation, and not to become religious leaders. If we do not know the true path, how can we lead others? We must seek out the Master Gautama, for he has attained the path we have long sought."

Sariputta and Moggallana prostrated themselves before Sanjaya and then departed, followed by the other parivrajakas. They walked to Palm Forest where they all prostrated before the Buddha and asked to be ordained. The Buddha spoke to them about the Four Noble Truths and accepted them as bhikkhus in his sangha. After the ordination ceremony, the number of bhikkhus in Palm Grove numbered 1,250.

On the full moon day, the Buddha took his bowl and entered the city of Rajagaha with his 1,250 bhikkhus. They walked silently with slow, calm steps. King Bimbisara came out to welcome the Buddha. He led the Buddha and the bhikkhus to the royal courtyard where spacious tents had been set up to shade the guests from the hot sun.

When the Buddha and all of the 1,250 bhikkhus had finished eating, their bowls were taken and washed and then returned. King Bimbisara turned toward the Buddha and joined his palms. Understanding the king's wishes, the Buddha began to teach the Dharma. He spoke about the five precepts as the way to create peace and happiness for one's family and all the kingdom.

"The first precept is: do not kill. Observing this precept nourishes compassion. All living beings fear death. As we cherish our own lives, we should cherish the lives of all other beings. Not only should we refrain from taking human life, we should strive to avoid taking the lives of other species. We must live in harmony with people, animals, and plants. If we nourish a heart of love, we can reduce suffering and create a happy life. If every citizen observes the precept not to kill, the kingdom will have peace. When the people respect each other's lives, the country will prosper and be strong, and it will be safe from invasion by other countries. Even if the kingdom possesses great military force, there will be no reason to use it. Soldiers can devote time to such worthy tasks as building roads, bridges, and marketplaces.

"The second precept is: do not steal. No one has the right to take away the possessions that another has earned by his own labor. Attempting to seize another's goods violates this precept. Do not cheat others or use your influence and power to encroach on other's goods. Making profits from the sweat and labor of others violates this precept, as well. If the citizens observe this precept, social equality will flower, and robbing and killing will quickly cease.

"The third precept is: avoid sexual misconduct. Sexual relations should only take place with your spouse. Observing this precept builds trust and happiness in the family, and prevents unnecessary suffering to others. If you want happiness, and the time and will to help your country and people, abstain from having several concubines.

"The fourth precept is: do not lie. Do not speak words that can create division and hatred. Your words should be in accord with the truth. Yes means yes. No means no. Words have the power to create trust and happiness, or they can create misunderstanding and hatred and even lead to murder and war. Please use words with the greatest care.

"The fifth precept is: do not drink alcohol or use other intoxicants. Alcohol and intoxicants rob the mind of clarity. When someone is intoxicated he can cause untold suffering to himself, his family, and others. Observing this precept is to preserve health for the body and mind. This precept should be observed at all times.

"If your majesty and all high-ranking officials study and observe these five precepts, the kingdom will benefit greatly. Your majesty, a king stands at the helm of his country. He must live with awareness and know all that is happening in his kingdom at all times. If you see to it that those under your charge understand and observe the five precepts, the five principles of living in peace and harmony, the country of Magadha will thrive."

Overcome with joy, King Bimbisara stood and bowed before the Buddha. Queen Videhi approached the Buddha, holding the hand of her son, Prince Ajatasattu. She showed the prince how to join his palms like a lotus bud and respectfully greet the Buddha. She said, "Lord Buddha, Prince Ajatasattu and four hundred other children are present today. Can you teach them about the Way of Awareness and Love?"

The queen bowed before the Buddha. The Buddha smiled. He reached out and clasped the young prince's hand. The queen turned around and motioned for the other children to come forward. They were the children of noble and wealthy families and were dressed in the finest of garments. Boys as well as girls wore golden bracelets around their wrists and ankles. The girls were dressed in shimmering saris of many colors. Prince Ajatasattu sat down by the feet of the Buddha. The Buddha thought of the poor country children he shared a picnic with so long ago beneath the rose-apple tree in Kapilavatthu. He silently promised himself that when he returned home he would seek out such children and share the teaching with them, too.

After the Buddha spoke to the children, King Bimbisara stood up, joined his palms and bowed, and said, "Master, our kingdom is blessed to have you among us. I would now like to present you and your sangha with a gift, if you agree." About two miles north of Rajagaha, there is a large and beautiful forest known as Venuvana, Bamboo Forest. It is quiet and serene, cool and refreshing. Many gentle squirrels inhabit that forest. I would like to offer Venuvana to you and your sangha as a place where you can teach and practice the Way.

"O Great Teacher of Compassion, please accept this gift from my heart." The Buddha reflected for a moment. It was the first time the sangha had been offered land for a monastery. Certainly his bhikkhus did need a place to dwell during the rainy season. The Buddha breathed deeply and smiled, and he nodded his head in acceptance of the king's generous gift. King Bimbisara was overjoyed. He knew that the presence of the monastery would mean that the Buddha would spend more time in Magadha.

The very next day, the Buddha visited Bamboo Forest with several of his senior students. It was an ideal location for the sangha, with nearly one hundred acres of healthy bamboo groves. Many kinds of bamboo grew there. At the center of the forest, Kalandaka Lake would be a perfect place for the bhikkhus to bathe, wash their robes, and do walking meditation along the shore. Because the bamboo was so plentiful, it would be easy to build small huts for the older monks to live in. The Buddha's senior students, including Kondanna, Kassapa, and Sariputta, were all delighted with Bamboo Forest. They began planning at once how to best organize a monastery there.

The Buddha said, "The monsoon season is not a good time for travel. The bhikkhus need a place to study and practice together during the rains. Having a place like this will help the community avoid illness from exposure to the elements and will also help them avoid stepping on the many worms and insects that are washed up on the ground during the rainy season. From now on, I would like the bhikkhus to return to a common place at the beginning of every rainy season. We can ask lay disciples of the area to bring food offerings during the three months of retreat. The lay disciples will also benefit from the teachings offered by the bhikkhus." Thus, the tradition of the rainy-season retreat began. The younger bhikkhus built huts from bamboo, thatch, and pounded earth for the Buddha and the older bhikkhus. Bhikkhu Nagasamala built a low, wooden platform for the Buddha to sleep upon. He also placed a large earthenware vessel for washing behind the Buddha's hut. Nagasamala was a young bhikkhu who had been Uruvela Kassapa's disciple. He was asked by Kassapa to serve as an attendant to the Buddha when the sangha moved to Bamboo Forest.

Lay disciples assisted in many ways. Kassapa proved to be as talented at organizing the laity as he was at organizing the bhikkhus. He met with lay sponsors of the monastery and helped them organize the food offerings and other forms of assistance. He assured that every bhikkhu received a robe, begging bowl, meditation cushion, towel, and water filter for personal use.

The Buddha sat in meditation far into the night. He liked to place his bamboo platform outside his hut and sit on it, enjoying the cool night air, especially on nights with a moon. Before dawn, he liked to do walking meditation around the lake. Ever joyous, peaceful, and relaxed, the Buddha did not require as much sleep as the younger bhikkhus.

King Bimbisara visited the Bamboo Forest faithfully. Sometimes he was accompanied by Queen Videhi and Prince Ajatasattu. Often he came alone. He would leave his carriage at the edge of the forest and walk on his own to the Buddha's hut. One day after seeing the bhikkhus listening to the Dharma talk in the rain, he asked the Buddha's permission to build a large Dharma hall where the bhikkhus could both eat and listen to the teachings without being drenched by the rain. The Buddha consented, and work on the hall began right away. It was large enough to shelter more than one thousand bhikkhus and one thousand lay disciples. The Dharma hall was a most helpful addition to the monastery.

The Buddha and the king often sat together on the bamboo platform while carrying on conversations. Then Nagasamala built some simple bamboo chairs to enable the Buddha to receive guests more easily. One day as the Buddha and the king sat on two of the chairs, the king confided, "I have another son that you have not yet met. I would like very much for you to meet him and his mother. He is not the child of Queen Videhi. His mother's name is Ambapali and his name is Jivaka. He will soon be sixteen years old. Ambapali lives in Vesali, north of the city Pataliputta. She does not like the confined life of the palace and she is not concerned about titles of prestige. She treasures only her own freedom. I have provided them with several means of support, including a beautiful mango grove. Jivaka is a diligent and intelligent boy who is not at all interested in military or political affairs. He is living near the capital, pursuing medical studies. I love them deeply and hope you will love them too. O Compassionate One, if you would agree to meet Jivaka and his mother, I will ask them to come to Bamboo Forest in the near future."

The Buddha quietly smiled in agreement. The king joined his palms and departed, his heart filled with gratitude.

During that same period, Bamboo Forest Monastery received two very special guests who had come all the way from Kapilavatthu, the Buddha's home. They were the Buddha's old friend, Kaludayi, and Channa, who had driven the Buddha's carriage. Their presence imparted a special warmth to the monastery.

The Buddha had been absent for more than seven years and he was anxious to hear news of home. He asked Kaludayi about the king and queen, Yasodhara, Nanda, Sundari Nanda, his friends, and of course, his son Rahula. Though Kaludayi was still hale and hearty, his face bore the lines of age. Channa looked older too. The Buddha spoke with them for a long time as they sat outside his hut. He learned that Kaludayi now held considerable rank at court and was one of King Suddhodana's most trusted advisors. News that the Buddha had attained the Way and was teaching in Magadha had reached Kapilavatthu two months previously. Everyone rejoiced at the news, especially the king and queen, and Gopa. The king, much to Kaludayi's pleasure, had sent Kaludayi to invite the Buddha to return home. He took three days to prepare for the journey, unable to sleep at night for sheer excitement. Yasodhara suggested he take Channa along. Channa was so happy when Kaludayi agreed that he openly wept. It took the two men nearly a month to reach Bamboo Forest Monastery.

The Buddha's heart was warmed by all the news of home. Finally, Kaludayi asked the Buddha when he might return to Kapilavatthu. The Buddha said, "I will return after the rainy season. I do not want to leave the young bhikkhus here until they are more firmly anchored in their practice. After this period of retreat, I will feel more at ease about leaving them. But Kaludayi! Channa! Why don't you remain here yourselves for a month or so to taste this life? That will still allow you plenty of time to return to Kapilavatthu and inform the king that I will be back after monsoon season."

Kaludayi and Channa were delighted to remain as guests at Bamboo Forest Monastery. They made friends with many of the bhikkhus and were able to taste the joyous and peaceful life of one who leaves home to follow the Way. They learned how practicing the way of awareness in daily life could nourish the mind and heart. Kaludayi spent much time at the Buddha's side and observed him carefully. He was deeply moved by the Buddha's wondrous ease. It was clear that the Buddha had attained a state in which he no longer chased after any desire. The Buddha was like a fish swimming freely, or a cloud floating peacefully in the sky. He dwelled completely in the present moment.

The Buddha's eyes and smile were evidence of the wonderful liberation his spirit enjoyed. Nothing in this world bound him, and yet no one else possessed so great an understanding and love for others as he did. Kaludayi saw that his old friend had left him far behind on the spiritual path. Suddenly, Kaludayi found himself longing for the serene, unfettered life of a bhikkhu. He felt ready to abandon all rank, wealth, and prestige, and all the worries and anxieties that accompanied such a life. After spending just seven days at Bamboo Forest, he confided his wish to be ordained as a bhikkhu to the Buddha. The Buddha looked somewhat surprised, but then he smiled and nodded his head in acceptance.

Channa felt the same desire to become a bhikkhu but, aware of his duty to the royal family, he reflected that he should not become a bhikkhu without first asking Yasodhara's leave. He resolved to wait until the Buddha returned to Kapilavatthu before making his request.

A person who only looks at the finger and mistakes it for the moon will never see the real moon.

CHAPTER THIRTEEN

The Finger is Not the Moon

One afternoon Sariputta and Moggallana brought a friend, the ascetic Dighanakha, to meet the Buddha. Dighanakha was as well known as Sanjaya. He also happened to be Sariputta's uncle. When he learned that his nephew had become a disciple of the Buddha, he was curious to learn about the Buddha's teaching. When he asked Sariputta and Moggallana to explain the teaching to him, they suggested he meet directly with the Buddha.

Dighanakha asked the Buddha, "Gautama, what is your teaching? What are your doctrines? For my own part, I dislike all doctrines and theories. I don't subscribe to any at all."

The Buddha smiled and asked, "Do you subscribe to your doctrine of not following any doctrines? Do you believe in your doctrine of not-believing?"

Somewhat taken aback, Dighanakha replied, "Gautama, whether I believe or don't believe is of no importance."

The Buddha spoke gently, "Once a person is caught by belief in a doctrine, he loses all his freedom. When one becomes dogmatic, he believes his doctrine is the only truth and that all other doctrines are heresy. Disputes and conflicts all arise from narrow views. They can extend endlessly, wasting precious time and sometimes even leading to war. Attachment to views is the greatest impediment to the spiritual path. Bound to narrow views, one becomes so entangled that it is no longer possible to let the door of truth open," he said.

"Let me tell you a story about a young widower who lived with his five-year-old son. He cherished his son more than his own life. One day he left his son at home while he went out on business. When he was gone, brigands came and robbed and burned the entire village. They kidnapped his son. When the man returned home, he found the charred corpse of a young child lying beside his burned house. He took it to be the body of his own son. He wailed in grief and cremated what was left of the corpse. Because he loved his son so dearly, he put the ashes in a bag which he carried with him everywhere he went. Several months later, his son managed to escape from the brigands and make his way home. He arrived in the middle of the night and knocked at the door. At that moment, the father was hugging the bag of ashes and weeping. He refused to open the door even when the child called out that he was the man's son. He believed that his own son was dead and that the child knocking at the door was some neighborhood child mocking his grief. Finally, his son had no choice but to wander off on his own. Thus father and son lost each other forever."

"You see, my friend, if we are attached to some belief and hold it to be the absolute truth, we may one day find ourselves in a similar situation as the young widower. Thinking that we already possess the truth, we will be unable to open our minds to receive the truth, even if truth comes knocking at our door."

Dighanakha asked, "But what of your own teaching? If someone follows your teaching, will he become caught in narrow views?"

"My teaching is not a doctrine or a philosophy. It is not the result of discursive thought or mental conjecture like various philosophies, which contend that the fundamental essence of the universe is fire, water, earth, wind, or spirit; or that the universe is either finite or infinite, temporal or eternal. Mental conjecture and discursive thought about the truth are like ants crawling around the rim of a bowl—they never get anywhere. My teaching is not a philosophy. It is the result of direct experience. The things I say come from my own experience. You can confirm them all by your own experience. I teach that all things are impermanent and without a separate self. This I have learned from my own direct experience. You can too. I teach that all things depend on all other things to arise, develop, and pass away. Nothing is created from a single, original source. I have directly experienced this truth, and you can also. My goal is not to explain the universe, but to help guide others to have a direct experience of reality. Words cannot describe reality. Only direct experience enables us to see the true face of reality."

Dighanakha exclaimed, "Wonderful, wonderful, Gautama! But what would happen if a person did perceive your teaching as a dogma?"

The Buddha was quiet for a moment and then nodded his head. "Dighanakha, that is a very good question. My teaching is not a dogma or a doctrine, but no doubt some people will take it as such. I must state clearly that my teaching is a method to experience reality and not reality itself, just as a finger pointing at the moon is not the moon itself. An intelligent person makes use of the finger to see the moon. A person who only looks at the finger and mistakes it for the moon will never see the real moon. My teaching is a means of practice, not something to hold on to or worship. My teaching is like a raft used to cross the river. Only a fool would carry the raft around after he had already reached the other shore, the shore of liberation."

Dighanakha joined his palms. "Please, Lord Buddha, show me how to be liberated from painful feelings."

The Buddha said, "There are three kinds of feelings—pleasant, unpleasant, and neutral. All three have roots in the perceptions of mind and body. Feelings arise and pass away like any other mental or material phenomena. I teach the method of looking deeply in order to illuminate the nature and source of feelings, whether they are pleasant, unpleasant, or neutral. When you can see the source of your feelings, you will understand their nature. You will see that feelings are impermanent, and gradually you will remain undisturbed by their arising and passing away. Almost all painful feelings have their source in an incorrect way of looking at reality. When you uproot erroneous views, suffering ceases. Erroneous views cause people to consider the impermanent to be permanent. Ignorance is the source of all suffering. We practice the way of awareness in order to overcome ignorance. One must look deeply into things in order to penetrate their true nature. One cannot overcome ignorance through prayers and offerings."

Sariputta, Moggallana, Kaludayi, Nagasamala, and Channa all listened as the Buddha explained these things to Dighanakha. Sariputta was able to grasp the meaning of the Buddha's words the most deeply. He felt his own mind shine like a bright sun. Unable to conceal his joy, he joined his palms and prostrated himself before the Buddha. Moggallana prostrated himself, as well. Then Dighanakha, moved and profoundly impressed by all that the Buddha had said, also prostrated himself before the Buddha. Kaludayi and Channa were deeply touched by this scene. They felt proud to be associated with the Buddha, and their faith and trust in his Way was further strengthened.

A few days after that, Queen Videhi and an attendant visited and made food offerings to the sangha. She also brought a young plumeria sapling and planted it beside the Buddha's hut in remembrance of a teaching-story he had told the children in the palace courtyard.

Under the Buddha's guidance, the community made ever greater progress along the path. Sariputta and Moggallana were like shining stars with their keen intelligence, diligence, and leadership abilities. They worked with Kondanna and Kassapa to organize and guide the sangha. However, even as the sangha's reputation was growing, some people began to speak ill of the Buddha and his community. Some of these rumors were spread by members of religious factions who were jealous of the king's support for the sangha. Lay disciples who often visited Bamboo Forest expressed concern over what was being said. Apparently, some people in Rajagaha were distressed that so many young men from wealthy and noble families had become bhikkhus. They feared that soon all the young men would abandon their homes and there would be no more suitable husbands for the noble young women in Rajagaha. Entire family lines could be discontinued, they warned.

Many bhikkhus were not pleased when they heard these things. But when the Buddha was informed, he calmed both the laity and the bhikkhus by saying, "Don't worry about such things. Sooner or later, all such talk will die down." And it did. In less than a month, there was no more talk about such trifling fears.

When the rainy-season retreat came to a close, the Buddha summoned Kaludayi and Channa and suggested they leave for Kapilavatthu first, in order to announce the Buddha's imminent arrival. Kaludayi and Channa made preparations for their trip without delay. Kaludayi, now a bhikkhu of calm and serene bearing, knew that everyone in the capital would be surprised when they saw him. He looked forward to the happy task of announcing the Buddha's return, but he regretted leaving Bamboo Forest after so brief a stay.

Yasodhara told Rahula, "Dear son, that monk is your own father."

CHAPTER FOURTEEN

Reunion

Kaludayi told the king, queen, and Yasodhara the news of the Buddha's imminent arrival, and then, taking just his begging bowl, set off alone to meet the Buddha on his way to Kapilavatthu. Kaludayi walked with the serene, slow steps of a bhikkhu. He walked days and rested nights, pausing only briefly in tiny hamlets along the way to beg for food. Wherever he went, he announced that Prince Siddhartha had found the Way and was about to return home. Nine days after he left Kapilavatthu, Kaludayi met the Buddha and three hundred bhikkhus traveling with him. Moggallana, Kondanna, and the Kassapa brothers had remained with the other bhikkhus in Bamboo Forest.

At Kaludayi's suggestion, the Buddha and his bhikkhus rested the night in Nigrodha Park, three miles south of Kapilavatthu. The following morning they entered the city to beg.

The sight of three hundred bhikkhus wearing saffron robes, peacefully and silently holding their bowls to beg, made a deep impression on the city's people. It did not take long for news of their arrival to reach the palace. King Suddhodana ordered a carriage be readied at once to take him out to meet his son. Queen Mahapajapati and Yasodhara waited anxiously within the palace.

When the king's carriage entered the eastern sector of the city, they encountered the bhikkhus. The carriage driver recognized Siddhartha first. "Your majesty, there he is! He walks ahead of the others and his robe is a bit longer."

Astonished, the king recognized that the bhikkhu clad in a saffron robe was indeed his own son. The Buddha radiated majesty and seemed almost surrounded by a halo of light. He was standing holding his bowl in front of a shabby dwelling. In his serene concentration, it appeared that the act of begging was at that moment the most important thing in his life. The king watched as a woman dressed in tattered clothes came out of the poor hut and placed a small potato in the Buddha's bowl. The Buddha respectfully received it by bowing to the woman. He then moved on to the next house.

The king's carriage was still some distance from where the Buddha stood. The king asked his driver to halt. He stepped out of the carriage and walked towards the Buddha. Just then, the Buddha saw his father approaching. They walked towards each other, the king with hurried steps, the Buddha with calm, relaxed steps.

"Siddhartha!"

"Father!"

Nagasamala came up to the Buddha and took his teacher's bowl, enabling the Buddha to hold the king's hands in his own two hands. Tears streamed down the king's wrinkled cheeks. The Buddha gazed at his father, his eyes filled with loving warmth. The king understood that Siddhartha was no longer the crown prince, but a respected spiritual teacher. He wanted to embrace Siddhartha but felt that it might not be proper. Instead he joined his palms and bowed to his son in the manner a king greets a high-ranking spiritual teacher.

The Buddha turned to Sariputta who was nearby and said, "The bhikkhus have completed their begging. Please lead them back to Nigrodha Park. Nagasamala will accompany me to the palace where we can eat our food. We will return to the sangha later in the afternoon."

Sariputta bowed and then turned to lead the others back to the park.

The king looked long and hard at the Buddha before saying, "I thought surely you would come to the palace to see your family first. Who could have guessed you would instead go begging in the city?

Why didn't you come to eat at the palace?"

The Buddha smiled at his father. "Father, I am not alone. I have traveled with a large community, the community of bhikkhus. I, too, am a bhikkhu and, like all other bhikkhus, I beg for my food."

"But must you beg for food at such poor dwellings as these around here? No one in the history of the Sakya clan has ever done such a thing."

Again the Buddha smiled. "Perhaps no Sakya has ever done so before, but all bhikkhus have. Father, begging is a spiritual practice which helps a bhikkhu develop humility and see that all persons are equal. When I receive a small potato from a poor family, it is no different than when I receive an elegant dish served by a king. A bhikkhu can transcend barriers that discriminate between rich and poor. On my path, all are considered equal. Everyone, no matter how poor he is, can attain liberation and enlightenment. Begging does not demean my own dignity. It recognizes the inherent dignity of all persons."

King Suddhodana listened with his mouth slightly agape. The old prophecies were true. Siddhartha had become a spiritual teacher whose virtue would shine throughout the world. Holding the king's hand, the Buddha walked with him back to the palace. Nagasamala followed them.

Thanks to a palace attendant who spotted the bhikkhus and called out, Queen Gotami, Yasodhara, Sundari Nanda, and young Rahula were able to watch the encounter between the king and the Buddha from a palace balcony. They saw how the king bowed to the Buddha. As the king and the Buddha neared the palace, Yasodhara turned to Rahula. She pointed to the Buddha and said, "Dear son, do you see that monk holding your grandfather's hand, about to enter the palace gates?" Rahula nodded.

"That monk is your own father. Run down and greet him. He has a very special inheritance to pass on to you. Ask him about it."

Rahula ran downstairs. In a flash, he reached the palace courtyard. He ran toward the Buddha. The Buddha knew at once that the little boy running toward him was Rahula. He opened his arms wide and embraced his son. Almost out of breath, Rahula gasped, "Respected monk, mother said I should ask you about my special inheritance. What is it? Can you show it to me?"

The Buddha patted Rahula's cheek and smiled. "You want to know about your inheritance? All in good time, I will pass it on to you."

The Buddha took the boy's hand in his, while still holding the king's hand. Together the three of them entered the palace.

Queen Gotami, Yasodhara, and Sundari Nanda came downstairs and saw the king, the Buddha, and Rahula entering the royal gardens. The spring sunshine was pleasantly warm. Flowers blossomed everywhere and birds warbled sweet songs. The Buddha sat down with the king and Rahula on a marble bench. He invited Nagasamala to be seated too. At that moment, Queen Gotami, Yasodhara, and Sundari Nanda entered the gardens.

The Buddha immediately stood up and walked toward the three women. Queen Gotami was a picture of good health. She wore a sari the color of cool green bamboo. Gopa was as beautiful as ever, although she appeared somewhat pale. Her sari was as white as fresh-fallen snow. She wore no jewels or ornaments. The Buddha's younger sister, now sixteen years old, wore a gold sari which set off her shining black eyes. The women joined their palms and bowed low to greet the Buddha. The Buddha joined his palms and bowed in return. Then he called out, "Mother! Gopa!"

Hearing his voice call out their names, both women began to weep.

The Buddha took the queen's hand and led her to sit down on a bench. He asked, "And where is my brother, Nanda?"

The queen answered, "He is out practicing martial arts. He should return soon. Do you recognize your younger sister? She has grown much in your absence, wouldn't you say?"

The Buddha gazed at his sister. He had not seen her in more than seven years. "Sundari Nanda, you're a young woman now!"

Then the Buddha approached Yasodhara and gently took her hand. She was so moved that her hand trembled in his. He led her to sit beside Queen Gotami, and then he sat back on his own bench. On the walk back to the palace, the king had asked the Buddha many questions, but now no one spoke, not even Rahula. The Buddha looked at the king and queen, Yasodhara, and Sundari Nanda. The joy of reunion shone in everyone's face. After a long silence, the Buddha spoke, "Father, I have returned. Mother, I have returned. See, Gopa, I came back to you."

Again the two women began to cry. Their tears were tears of joy. The Buddha let them silently weep, and then he asked Rahula to sit beside him. He patted the boy's hair affectionately.

Gotami wiped her tears with the edge of her sari, and, smiling at the Buddha, said, "You were gone a very long time. More than seven years have passed. Do you understand how courageous a woman Gopa has been?"

"I have long understood the depth of her courage, Mother. You and Yasodhara are the two most courageous women I know. Not only have you offered understanding and support to your husbands, but also you are models of strength and determination for all. I have been very lucky to have both of you in my life. It has made my task much easier."

Yasodhara smiled but she did not speak.

The king said, "You have told me a bit about your search for the Way up to your ordeals of self-mortification. Could you repeat all you have told me for the others to hear and then continue?"

The Buddha told them about his long search for the Way in brief. He told them about meeting King Bimbisara on the mountain, and about the poor children of Uruvela village. He told them about his five friends who had practiced austerities with him, and about the great reception the bhikkhus received in Rajagaha. Everyone listened intently. Not even Rahula budged.

The Buddha's voice was warm and affectionate. He did not dwell on details and he spoke only sparingly of his period of self-mortification. He used his words to sow helpful seeds of awakening in the hearts of those closest to him.

An attendant came out to the garden and whispered something in Gotami's ear. The queen whispered something back. Soon after, the attendant prepared a table in the garden for the noon meal. Just as the food was being placed upon the table, Nanda arrived. The Buddha greeted him joyfully.

"Nanda! When I left you were only fifteen. Now you're a grown man!" Nanda smiled. The queen chastised him, "Nanda, greet your elder brother properly. He is a monk now. Join your palms and bow."

Nanda bowed and the Buddha bowed to his younger brother in return. They all moved to the table. The Buddha asked Nagasamala to sit beside him. A serving maid brought out water for everyone to wash their hands.

The king asked the Buddha, "What did you receive in your begging bowl?"

"I received a potato, but I notice that Nagasamala did not yet receive anything."

King Suddhodana stood up. "Please allow me to offer both of you food from our table." Yasodhara held the platters while the king served the two bhikkhus. He placed fragrant white rice and vegetable curry into their bowls. The Buddha and Nagasamala ate in silent mindfulness and the others followed their example. Birds continued to sing throughout the garden.

When they had finished eating, the queen invited the king and the Buddha to sit again on the marble benches. A servant brought out a platter of tangerines, but Rahula was the only one to eat his. Everyone else was too absorbed in listening to the Buddha recount his experiences. Queen Gotami asked more questions than anyone else. When the king heard about the hut the Buddha lived in at Bamboo Forest, he resolved to have a similar one built at Nigrodha Park for him. He expressed his hope that the Buddha would remain for several months in order to teach them the Way. Queen Gotami, Yasodhara, Nanda, and Sundari Nanda voiced their joyous approval of the king's suggestion.

At last the Buddha said it was time for him to return to his bhikkhus in the park. The king rose and said, "I would like to invite you and all the bhikkhus for a meal offering just as the king of Magadha did. I will invite all the royal family and members of the government at the same time so that they can hear you speak about the Way."

The Buddha said he would be glad to accept the invitation. They arranged for the gathering to take place in seven days. Yasodhara expressed a desire to invite the Buddha, Nagasamala, and Kaludayi for a private meal with herself and Queen Gotami in the eastern palace. The Buddha accepted her invitation, as well, but suggested it would be best to wait until a few days after the king's reception.

The king wanted to order a carriage to take the Buddha and Nagasamala back to Nigrodha Park, but the Buddha refused. He explained that he preferred to travel by foot. The entire family accompanied the two bhikkhus to the palace's outer gates. They all joined their palms respectfully and bid the two bhikkhus farewell.

Nigrodha Park was soon transformed into a monastery. The ancient fig trees that grew there provided cool shade. Many new bhikkhus were ordained, and many laypersons, including a number of young people of the Sakya clan, took the five precepts.

Yasodhara made frequent visits to the Buddha at Nigrodha Park, accompanied by the queen and young Rahula. She listened to his Dharma talks and in private asked him about the relation between practicing the Way and performing social service. The Buddha showed her how to observe her breath and practice meditation in order to nourish peace and joy in her own heart. She understood that without peace and joy, she could not truly help others. She learned that by developing deeper understanding, she could deepen her capacity to love. She was happy to discover that she could practice the way of awareness in the very midst of her efforts to serve others. Peace and joy were possible right in the very moments she was working. Means and ends were not two different things.

CHAPTER FIFTEEN

A New Faith

Two weeks after the private meal in Princess Yasodhara's palace, King Suddhodana invited the Buddha to a meal at his own palace. Sariputta was also invited. Queen Gotami, Yasodhara, Nanda, Sundari Nanda, and Rahula were all present. In the close-knit atmosphere of his family, the Buddha showed them how to follow their breath, how to look deeply into their feelings, and how to do walking and sitting meditation. He emphasized how they could transcend the worries, frustrations, and irritations of daily life by practicing mindfulness in daily life.

Rahula sat next to Sariputta and placed his small hand in the elder monk's hand. Rahula was very fond of Sariputta.

When the time came for the Buddha and Sariputta to return to the monastery, everyone walked with them to the gate. Nanda held the Buddha's bowl as the Buddha joined his palms and bowed farewell to each person. To Nanda's surprise, the Buddha did not take his bowl back. Not knowing what to do, Nanda followed the Buddha back to the monastery waiting for the right moment to return the bowl. When they arrived at the monastery, the Buddha asked Nanda if he would like to spend a week at the monastery to enjoy a deeper taste of the life of a bhikkhu. Nanda loved and respected his elder brother, and so he agreed. Nanda felt drawn to the calm and relaxed life of the bhikkhus he saw around him. When the Buddha asked him at the end of the week if he would like to be ordained and live a bhikkhu's life for several months under the Buddha's guidance, Nanda was most willing. The Buddha asked Sariputta to give Nanda basic instruction and to ordain him as a bhikkhu.

The Buddha had first consulted with his father, the king, about allowing Nanda to live as a bhikkhu for a period of time. The king agreed with the Buddha that while Nanda was a well-meaning young man, he lacked the strength of character and determination required of a future king. The Buddha said he could provide Nanda with training that would help Nanda build clarity and resolve. The king was in agreement.

Less than a month passed, however, when Nanda began to pine away for his fiancée, the beautiful Janapada Kalyani. He tried to conceal his longing, but the Buddha saw clearly into his feelings. One day the Buddha said to Nanda, "If you want to realize your goal, you must first overcome clinging to ordinary emotions. Devote your whole self to your practice and train your mind. Only then can you become an effective leader who can serve others well."

The Buddha asked Sariputta to see that Nanda was no longer sent to do his begging in Kalyani's neighborhood. When Nanda learned of this, he felt a mixture of both resentment and gratitude to the Buddha. He understood that the Buddha could see into his deepest thoughts and needs.

Rahula envied his young uncle for being able to live at the monastery. He wanted to be allowed to do the same. But when he asked his mother, she patted his head and said that he must first grow much bigger before he could become a monk. Rahula asked how he could grow faster. She told him to eat well and exercise each day.

One day when she saw the bhikkhus begging close to the palace, Yasodhara turned to Rahula and said, "Why don't you run down and greet the Buddha? Ask him again about your inheritance."

Rahula ran downstairs. He loved his mother dearly, but he also loved his father. He had spent all his days with his mother, but had never spent even one whole day with his father. He wished he could be like Nanda and live by the Buddha's side. He ran quickly across the courtyard and out the south gate until he caught up with the Buddha. The Buddha smiled and extended his hand. Though the spring sun was already growing hot, Rahula felt protected by his father's shadow and love. He looked up at his father and said, "It is very cool and refreshing by your side."

Rahula asked the Buddha, "What is my inheritance?"

The Buddha answered, "Come to the monastery, and I will transmit it to you."

Yasodhara watched them from the palace balcony. She knew that the Buddha had given Rahula permission to return with him to the monastery for the day.

When they returned to the monastery, Sariputta shared his food with Rahula. Rahula ate in silence as he sat between the Buddha and Sariputta. He was glad to see his uncle Nanda. The Buddha told Rahula that he could sleep overnight in Sariputta's hut. All the bhikkhus were fond of Rahula and treated him so warmly; Rahula wished he could live at the monastery forever. But Sariputta explained to him that if he wanted to stay at the monastery, he would have to become a monk. Rahula clasped Sariputta's hand and asked if he could ask the Buddha to ordain him. The Buddha agreed and instructed Sariputta to ordain the young boy.

At first Sariputta thought the Buddha was jesting, but when he saw how serious the Buddha was, he asked, "But, Master, how can one so young become a bhikkhu?"

The Buddha answered, "We will allow him to practice in preparation for full vows in the future. Let him take the vows of a novice for now. He can be given the task of chasing away the crows that disturb the bhikkhus during sitting meditation."

Sariputta shaved Rahula's head and gave him the three refuges. He taught Rahula four precepts: do not kill; do not steal; do not speak falsehoods; and do not drink alcohol. He took one of his own robes and cut it down to size for Rahula. He showed Rahula how to wear it and how to hold the bowl for begging. Rahula looked just like a miniature bhikkhu. He slept in Sariputta's hut and went begging with him each day in the small hamlets that bordered the monastery. Although the older bhikkhus ate only one meal a day, Sariputta feared Rahula would lack adequate nutrition for his growing body, and so he let the boy eat an evening meal, too. Lay disciples remembered to bring milk and extra food for the little monk.

When the news that Rahula had shaved his head and put on a bhikkhu's robe reached the palace, King Suddhodana was very upset. Both the king and queen missed Rahula terribly. They had expected him to visit the monastery for just a few days and then return to the palace. They hadn't dreamed he might remain in the monastery as a novice. They were lonely without their grandson. Yasodhara felt a mixture of sadness and happiness. Though she missed her son intensely, she was comforted to know he was now close to his father after not seeing him for so many years.

One afternoon, the king mounted his royal carriage with Queen Gotami and Yasodhara, and paid a visit to the monastery. They were met by the Buddha, Nanda, and Rahula. In his excitement, Rahula ran to his mother, and Yasodhara embraced her son warmly. Then Rahula hugged both his grandparents.

The king bowed to the Buddha and then said rather reproachfully, "I suffered unbelievably when you abandoned home to become a monk. Not long ago, Nanda left me as well. It is too much to bear to lose Rahula. For a family man like myself, the bonds between father and son, and grandfather and grandson are very important. The pain I felt when you left was like a knife cutting into my skin. After cutting into my skin, the knife cut into my flesh. After cutting into my flesh, the knife has cut clear to the bone. I beseech you to consider your actions. In the future, you should not allow a child to be ordained unless he has received prior approval by his parents."

The Buddha listened deeply and tried to comfort the king by speaking about the truths of impermanence and the absence of a separate self.

He reminded him that the daily practice of mindfulness was the only gate by which suffering could be overcome. Nanda and Rahula now had a chance to deeply live such a life. The Buddha encouraged his father to appreciate their good fortune and to continue to practice the way of awareness in daily life in order to find true happiness.

The king felt his pain lighten. Gotami and Yasodhara were also comforted and reassured by the Buddha's words.

Later that day, the Buddha said to Sariputta, "From now on, we will not receive children into the community of bhikkhus without the approval of their parents. Please note that in our monastic code."

Time passed quickly. The Buddha and his sangha had rested in the kingdom of Sakya for more than six months. New ordinations had increased the number of bhikkhus to more than five hundred. The number of lay disciples was too great to be counted. King Suddhodana also gave the sangha another place to build a monastery—the former summer palace of Prince Siddhartha, north of the capital, with its cool and spacious gardens. Venerable Sariputta organized a large number of bhikkhus to set up monastic living there. The presence of this new monastery helped assure a firm foundation for the practice of the Way in the Sakya kingdom.

The Buddha wished to return to Bamboo Forest in time for the rainy-season retreat, as he had promised King Bimbisara and the bhikkhus who had remained there. King Suddhodana invited the Buddha for a last meal before his departure and asked him to give a discourse on the Dharma for the royal family and all members of the Sakya clan.

The Buddha used this occasion to speak about applying the Way to political life. He said the Way could illuminate the realm of politics, assisting those involved in governing the kingdom to bring about social equality and justice.

"If you practice the Way, you will increase your understanding and compassion and better serve the people. You will find ways to bring about peace and happiness without depending on violence at all. You do not need to kill, torture, or imprison people, or confiscate property. This is not an impossible ideal, but something that can be actually realized.

"When a politician possesses enough understanding and love, he sees the truth about poverty, misery, and oppression. Such a person can find the means to reform the government in order to reduce the gap between rich and poor, and cease the use of force against others.

"My friends, political leaders and rulers must set an example. Don't live in the lap of luxury because wealth only creates a greater barrier between you and the people. Live a simple, wholesome life, using your time to serve the people, rather than pursuing idle pleasures. A leader cannot earn the trust and respect of his people if he does not set a good example. If you love and respect the people, they will love and respect you in return. Rule by virtue differs from rule by law and order. Rule by virtue does not depend on punishment. According to the Way of Awakening, true happiness can only be attained by the path of virtue."

King Suddhodana and all those present listened intently to the Buddha. Prince Dronodanaraja, the Buddha's uncle and the father of Devadatta and Ananda, said, "Rule by virtue, as you have described it, is truly beautiful. But I believe that you alone possess the character and virtue needed to realize such a path. Why don't you stay in Kapilavatthu and help create a new form of government right here in Sakya kingdom which will bring peace, joy, and happiness to all the people?"

King Suddhodana added, "I am old. If you agree to remain, I will gladly abdicate the throne in your favor. With your virtue, integrity, and intelligence, I am sure all the people will stand behind you. Before long our country will prosper as it never has before."

The Buddha smiled and did not speak right away. Looking kindly at his father, he said, "Father, I am no longer the son of one family, one clan, or even one country. My family is now all beings; my home is the Earth; and my position is that of a monk who depends on the generosity of others. I have chosen this path, not the path of politics. I believe I can best serve all beings in this way."

Although Queen Gotami and Yasodhara did not think it befitting to express their own views during this gathering, they were both moved to tears by the Buddha's words. They knew what he said was correct.

The Buddha continued speaking to the king and all those present about the five precepts and how to apply them in family life and society. The five precepts were the foundation of a happy family and a peaceful society. He explained each precept carefully, and concluded by saying, "If you want the people to be united, you must first obtain their faith and trust. If political leaders practice the five precepts, the people's faith and trust will grow. With that faith and trust, there is nothing the country can't accomplish. Peace, happiness, and social equality will be assured. Create a life based on awareness. The dogmas of the past do not build faith and trust nor do they encourage equality among the people. Let the Way of Awakening offer a new path and a new faith."

The Buddha assured them that although he would soon be departing for Magadha, he would return to Kapilavatthu in the future. The king and all those present were glad to hear that.

Meanwhile, a young man from a wealthy Sakyan family left home to find the Buddha and become a bhikkhu. His name was Anuruddha, and he persuaded a number of Sakyan princes to ordain with him. They were Bhagu, Kimbila, Devadatta, Ananda, and also Baddhiya who gave up his post as governor of the northern provinces. On the way, they were joined a young barber, Upali, who then became the first untouchable ordained by the Buddha.

The Buddha went from Magadha to the Bamboo Forest at Rajagaha for the rainy-season retreat. During the retreat, the Buddha ordained many new bhikkhus, among them Mahakassapa, a talented young man of rare depth. He and his wife both longed to follow the spiritual path. When Mahakassapa saw the Buddha, he knew he had found his true teacher. Mahakassapa told the Buddha of his wife's longing to become a nun and follow the Way, but the Buddha answered that the time was not yet ripe to admit women into the sangha and she would have to wait a little longer.

CHAPTER SIXTEEN

Cover the Land in Gold

Three days after the rainy season ended, a young man named Sudatta paid a visit to the Buddha to ask if he would come teach the Way of Awakening in Kosala. Sudatta was an extremely wealthy merchant. He lived in the capital city, Savatthi, in the kingdom of Kosala which was ruled by King Pasenadi. Sudatta was known to the people in his country as a philanthropist who always set aside a generous portion of his income to share with orphans and the destitute. His charitable efforts gave him much satisfaction and happiness. His people called him "Anathapindika," which means "the one who cares for the poor and abandoned."

Sudatta traveled frequently to Magadha to buy and sell goods. When in Rajagaha, he stayed with his wife's elder brother, who was also a merchant. He was staying with his brother-in-law at the end of the rainy season when one day his brother-in-law said, "Tomorrow I have invited the Buddha and his bhikkhus for a meal." Sudatta asked, with some surprise, "Doesn't 'Buddha' mean 'one who is awake?'"

"That is right. The Buddha is an awakened person, an enlightened master. Tomorrow you will have a chance to meet him."

He couldn't explain why, but just hearing the name Buddha filled Sudatta with happiness and inspiration. He asked to hear more about this enlightened teacher. The brother-in-law explained how after watching the serene bhikkhus beg in the city, he had gone to hear the Buddha at Bamboo Forest Monastery. He had become one of the Buddha's lay disciples and had even built a number of thatched huts at the monastery as an offering, in order to protect the bhikkhus from the sun and rain.

Perhaps, Sudatta marveled, it was from a past-life connection, but he felt great love and respect for the Buddha within his heart. He couldn't wait until the following day to meet the Buddha. He spent a restless night, anxiously waiting for daybreak so that he could pay a morning visit to Bamboo Forest Monastery. Unable to sleep any more, he got up even though the sky was still dark. The air was cold and misty. He made his way to Bamboo Forest. By the time he arrived, the first rays of morning sunlight were shining on the bamboo leaves. Though he wanted nothing more than to meet the Buddha, he felt somewhat nervous. To calm himself, he whispered, "Sudatta, do not worry."

At that very moment, the Buddha, who was doing walking meditation, passed Sudatta. He stopped and said softly, "Sudatta."

Sudatta joined his palms and bowed before the Buddha. They walked to the Buddha's hut, and Sudatta asked the Buddha if he had slept well. The Buddha replied he had. Sudatta told the Buddha how restless a night he had spent, so anxious was he to come and meet the Buddha. He asked the Buddha to teach him the Way. The Buddha spoke to Sudatta about understanding and love.

Sudatta was filled with great happiness. He prostrated before the Buddha and asked to become a lay disciple. The Buddha accepted him. Sudatta also invited the Buddha and all his bhikkhus to come have a meal the following day at the home of his brother-in-law.

After the meal offering, Sudatta knelt down and said, "Lord Buddha, the people of Kosala have not yet had an opportunity to welcome you and your sangha and to learn the Way of Awakening. Please consider my invitation for you to come to Kosala and spend a period of time. Please show compassion to the people of Kosala."

The Buddha agreed to discuss the idea with his senior disciples. He promised to give Sudatta a response within a few days.

A few days later, Sudatta visited Bamboo Forest Monastery and received the happy news that the Buddha had decided to accept his invitation. Sudatta assured the Buddha that he would find a suitable place for the Sangha and would provide for all their needs while they were there. Sudatta also suggested that the Buddha allow Venerable Sariputta to come to Kosala with him first in order to assist in preparations for the Buddha's arrival.

A week later, Sudatta and Sariputta set off together, crossing the Ganga and traveling to Vesali. They rested the night in Ambapali's mango grove. After bidding farewell to Ambapali, they headed northwest along the banks of the Aciravati River. Sudatta had never walked such distances before, having always used a carriage in the past.

Kosala was a large and prosperous kingdom, no less powerful than Magadha. Its southern border was marked by the Ganga and its northern border brushed the feet of the Himalayas. Sudatta, or Anathapindika, was known to everyone wherever he went. The people trusted what he told them, and they all looked forward to meeting the Buddha and his sangha. Every morning when Venerable Sariputta went begging, Sudatta accompanied him to speak to as many people as he could about the Buddha.

They reached Savatthi after a month. Sudatta invited Sariputta to his home for a meal and introduced him to his parents and wife. He asked Sariputta to speak about the Dharma, after which his parents and wife asked to take the three refuges and five precepts. Sudatta's wife was a lovely and graceful woman. Her name was Pimnalakkhana. They had four children—three girls and a boy. The daughters were named Subhadra Elder, Subhadra Younger, and Sumagadha. Their son, the youngest child, was named Kala.

Sariputta begged every morning in the city and slept in the forest by the banks of the river at night. Sudatta lost no time in searching for a place to host the Buddha and the bhikkhus.

Of all the places Sudatta visited, none was more beautiful and peaceful than the park belonging to Prince Jeta. He felt sure it would serve as the perfect place from which the Buddha's Way of Awakening could be spread to all corners of the kingdom. Sudatta went to see Prince Jeta and found him entertaining a palace official. Sudatta respectfully greeted them both and then expressed directly his hope that the prince would sell him the park to provide a practice center for the Buddha. The prince replied, "My father King Pasenadi gave me the park. I am very attached to it. I would only part with it if you agreed to cover every square inch of it in gold coins."

Sudatta responded, "Agreed, I will meet your price. Tomorrow I will have the gold brought to the park."

Prince Jeta was startled. "But I was only joking. I don't want to sell my park."

Sudatta answered with resolve, "Honorable Prince, you are a member of the royal family. You must carry out the words you have spoken."

Prince Jeta submitted, but he secretly hoped Sudatta would not be able to meet his price. Sudatta bowed and departed. Early the next morning, he sent great carts of gold coins and had his servants spread it over the entire park.

Prince Jeta was astounded when he saw the great mounds of gold. This Buddha and his sangha must be truly extraordinary for the young merchant to go to such lengths. The prince asked Sudatta to tell him about the Buddha. Sudatta's eyes shone as he spoke about his Teacher, the Dharma, and the sangha. He promised that he would bring Venerable Sariputta to meet the prince the following day. Prince Jeta found himself moved by the things Sudatta told him about the Buddha. He looked up to see that Sudatta's men had already spread gold coins over two thirds of the forest. Just as a fourth cart was arriving, he held out his hand and stopped them.

He said to Sudatta, "That is enough gold. Let the remaining land be my gift. I want to contribute to this beautiful project of yours."

Sudatta was pleased to hear this. When he brought Sariputta to meet the prince, the prince was impressed by the bhikkhu's peaceful bearing. Together they went to visit the park, which Sudatta had decided to call "Jetavana," or "Jeta Grove," in honor of the prince. Sudatta suggested to Sariputta that he live at Jetavana to help direct the building of the monastery. He said his family could bring food offerings to Sariputta each day. Together Sudatta, Sariputta, and the prince discussed building huts, a Dharma hall, a meditation hall, and bathrooms. They selected an especially cool and tranquil spot to build the Buddha's thatched hut. They oversaw the making of pathways and the digging of wells.

Sariputta began to give Dharma talks at Jetavana and the number of people who attended grew daily. Though none of the people had yet met the Buddha, they all felt drawn to his teaching.

Four months later, the monastery was nearly completed. Sariputta set off for Rajagaha in order to lead the Buddha and the bhikkhus back to Jetavana. He met them in the streets of Vesali and learned that they were dwelling nearby at Great Forest.

Ambapali was happy for the chance to offer the Buddha and his bhikkhus a meal in her mango grove. She only regretted that her son, Jivaka, was unable to attend because of his medical studies. On her way home from visiting the Buddha, her carriage was stopped by several princes of the Licchavi clan, the most powerful and wealthy lords in Vesali. They asked her where she was going, and she replied she was on her way home to prepare to receive the Buddha and his bhikkhus. After their encounter with her, then princes decided to go and see this teacher who was so highly respected by Ambapali. They left their carriages at the entrance to Great Forest and walked in.

The Buddha could tell that these young men possessed many seeds of compassion and wisdom. He invited them to be seated and he told them about his own life and search for the Way. He told them about the path to overcome suffering and realize liberation. He knew they belonged to the same warrior caste he had belonged to and looking at them, he could see himself as a young man. He spoke to them with warm understanding.

Their hearts were opened by the Buddha's words. They felt they could see themselves for the first time. They understood that wealth and power were not enough to bring them true happiness. They knew they had found a path for their lives. They all asked to be accepted as lay disciples. They entreated the Buddha to come dwell in Vesali the following year. They promised to build a monastery in Great Forest where several hundred bhikkhus could dwell. The Buddha accepted their proposal.

Ambapali visited the Buddha early the next morning and expressed her desire to offer the mango grove to the Buddha and his sangha. The Buddha accepted her gift. Shortly afterward, the Buddha, Sariputta, and three hundred bhikkhus headed north for Savatthi.

The road to Savatthi was now familiar to Sariputta. Because he and Anathapindika had nourished people's interest in the Buddha and the sangha, they were greeted warmly wherever they went. At nights the bhikkhus rested in the cool forests along the banks of the Aciravati River. The bhikkhus maintained peaceful serenity as they walked. Sometimes local people gathered in the forests or along the riverbanks to listen to the Buddha's teaching.

The day they arrived in Savatthi, they were greeted by Sudatta and Prince Jeta who took them to the new monastery. Seeing how well planned Jetavana was, the Buddha praised Sudatta. Sudatta responded by saying it was all thanks to the ideas and labor of Venerable Sariputta and Prince Jeta.

Prince Jeta and Sudatta arranged a reception immediately after the Buddha's arrival. Prince Jeta had come to deeply admire the Buddha through his contacts with Venerable Sariputta. They invited all the local people to come to hear the Buddha speak on the Dharma. Many came, including Price Jeta's mother, Queen Mallika, and his sixteen-year-old sister, Princess Vajiri. After hearing about the Buddha for months, everyone was most anxious to see him in person. The Buddha spoke about the Four Noble Truths and the Noble Eightfold Path.

After hearing the Dharma talk, the queen and princess felt their hearts open. They both wanted to become lay disciples, but did not dare to ask. The queen wanted to first seek the approval of her husband, King Pasenadi. She was sure that in the near future the king would meet the

Buddha and share her feelings. Pasenadi's own sister, who was King Bimbisara's wife, had already taken the three refuges with the Buddha three years before.

When the reception and Dharma talk were over, Sudatta respectfully knelt before the Buddha and said, "My family and I, together with all our friends and relations, offer Jetavana monastery to you and your sangha." The Buddha said, "Sudatta, your merit is great. Thanks to you, the sangha will be protected from sun and rain, wild animals, snakes, and mosquitoes. This monastery will draw bhikkhus from all four directions, now and in the future. You have supported the Dharma with all your heart. I hope you will continue to devote yourself to practicing the Way."

Once a week the Buddha gave a Dharma talk at Jetavana. Great numbers of people attended. Thus, it was not long before King Pasenadi was well aware of the impact of the Buddha's presence. King Pasenadi had a hard time believing that a monk as young as the Buddha could have achieved true enlightenment. According to the prince, the Buddha was thirty-nine years old, the same age as the king. He decided that when an occasion arose he would go and meet the Buddha himself.

The rainy season was approaching and the Buddha decided to spend it at Jetavana. Thanks to the experience gained during previous rainy seasons at Bamboo Forest, the Buddha's senior disciples organized the retreat with ease. Sixty new bhikkhus joined the community in Savatthi. Sudatta also introduced many friends who became lay disciples and enthusiastically supported the activities of the monastery.

One afternoon, the Buddha received a young man whose face was lined with grief and misery. The Buddha learned that the man had recently lost his only son and for several days had stood in the cemetery crying out loud, "My son, my son, where have you gone?" The man was unable to eat, drink, or sleep.

The Buddha told him, "In love, there is suffering."

The man objected, "You are wrong. Love doesn't cause suffering. Love brings only happiness and joy."

The bereaved man abruptly left before the Buddha could explain what he had meant. The man wandered aimlessly about until he stopped to chat with a group of men gambling in the street. He told them of his encounter with the Buddha. The men agreed with him that the Buddha was mistaken.

"How can love cause suffering? Love brings only happiness and joy! You're right. That monk Gautama was wrong."

Before long, news of this story spread throughout Savatthi and became a subject for heated debate. Many spiritual leaders contended that the Buddha was wrong about love. This matter reached the ears of King Pasenadi and that evening during the family meal, he said to the queen, "The monk the people call 'Buddha' may not be as great a teacher as the people seem to think he is."

The queen asked, "What makes you say that? Has someone said something bad about Teacher Gautama?"

"This morning, I heard some palace officials discussing Gautama. They said that according to him, the more you love the more you suffer."

The queen said, "If Gautama said that, it is undoubtedly true."

The king retorted impatiently, "You shouldn't speak like that. Examine things for yourself. Don't be like some small child who believes everything the teacher says."

The queen said no more. She knew that the king had not yet met the Buddha. The next morning she asked a close friend, the brahman Nalijangha, to visit the Buddha and ask him whether or not he had said that love was the source of suffering, and if he had to explain why. She asked her friend to note carefully everything the Buddha said and report back to her.

Nalijangha went to see the Buddha and asked him the queen's question. The Buddha responded, "Recently I heard that a woman in Savatthi lost her mother. She was so grief-stricken that she lost her mind and has been wandering the streets asking everyone, 'Have you seen my mother? Have you seen my mother?' I also heard about two young lovers who committed suicide together because the girl's parents were forcing her to marry someone else. These two stories alone demonstrate that love can cause suffering."

Nalijangha repeated the Buddha's words to Queen Mallika. One day soon after that she caught the king in a moment of leisure, and she asked him, "My husband, do you not love and cherish Princess Vajiri?"

"Indeed I do," answered the king, surprised by the question.

"If some misfortune befell her, would you suffer?"

The king was startled. Suddenly he saw clearly that the seeds of suffering existed within love. His sense of well-being was replaced with worry. The Buddha's words contained a cruel truth, which greatly disturbed the king. He said, "I will go visit this monk Gautama as soon as I have a chance."

"Lord, I do not dare come closer. I am an untouchable."

CHAPTER SEVENTEEN

Everyone's Tears Are Salty

King Pasenadi's visit to Jetavana stirred interest among the people and added to the stature of the Buddha's sangha. Palace officials noticed how King Pasenadi did not miss a single weekly Dharma talk, and many of them began to join him. Some did so out of admiration for the Buddha's teaching, while others went only in hopes of pleasing the king. The number of intellectuals and young people visiting Jetavana also mounted daily. During the three months of retreat, Sariputta ordained more than a hundred and fifty young men. Religious leaders of other sects that had long enjoyed the king's patronage began to feel threatened, and some of them began to regard Jetavana Monastery with less than sympathetic eyes. The retreat season concluded with a large service at which the king offered new robes to every bhikkhu and distributed food and other basic necessities to poor families. At this ceremony, the king and his family formally took the three refuges.

After the retreat, the Buddha and other bhikkhus traveled to neighboring regions in order to spread the Dharma to more and more people. One day, as the Buddha and bhikkhus were begging in a village near the banks of the Ganga, the Buddha spotted a man carrying night soil. The man was an untouchable named Sunita. Sunita had heard about the Buddha and bhikkhus, but this was the first time he had ever seen them. He was alarmed, knowing how dirty his clothes were and how foul he smelled from carrying night soil. He quickly moved off the path and made his way down to the river. But the Buddha was determined to share the Way with Sunita. When Sunita veered from the path, the Buddha did the same. Understanding the Buddha's intent, Sariputta and Meghiya, the Buddha's attendant at the time, followed him. The rows of other bhikkhus came to a halt and they quietly watched.

Sunita was panic-stricken. He hastily put the buckets of night soil down and looked for a place to hide. Above him stood the bhikkhus in their saffron robes, while before him approached the Buddha and two other bhikkhus. Not knowing what else to do, Sunita waded up to his knees in water and stood with his palms joined.

Curious villagers came out of their homes and lined the shore to watch what was happening. Sunita had veered off the path because he was afraid he would pollute the bhikkhus. He could not have guessed the Buddha would follow him. Sunita knew that the sangha included many men from noble castes. He was sure that polluting a bhikkhu was an unforgivable act. He hoped the Buddha and bhikkhus would leave him and return to the road. But the Buddha did not leave. He walked right up to the water's edge and said, "My friend, please come closer so we may talk."

Sunita, his palms still joined, protested, "Lord, I don't dare!"

"Why not?" asked the Buddha.

"I am an untouchable. I don't want to pollute you and your monks."

The Buddha replied, "On our path, we no longer distinguish between castes. You are a human being like the rest of us. We are not afraid we will be polluted. Only greed, hatred, and delusion can pollute us. A person as pleasant as yourself brings us nothing but happiness. What is your name?"

"Lord, my name is Sunita."

"Sunita, would you like to become a bhikkhu like the rest of us?"

"I couldn't!"

"Why not?"

"I'm an untouchable!"

"Sunita, I have already explained that on our path there is no caste.

In the Way of Awakening, caste no longer exists. It is like the Ganga, Yamuno, Aciravati, Sarabhu, Mahi, and Rohini rivers. Once they empty into the sea, they no longer retain their separate identities. A person who leaves home to follow the Way leaves caste behind whether he was born a brahman, *ksatriya, vaisya, sudra,* or untouchable. Sunita, if you like, you can become a bhikkhu like the rest of us."

Sunita could hardly believe his ears. He placed his joined palms before his forehead and said, "No one has ever spoken so kindly to me before. This is the happiest day of my life. If you accept me as your disciple, I vow to devote all my being to practicing your teaching."

The Buddha handed his bowl to Meghiya and reached his hand out to Sunita. He said, "Sariputta! Help me bathe Sunita. We will ordain him as a bhikkhu right here on the bank of the river."

Venerable Sariputta smiled. He placed his own bowl on the ground and came forward to assist the Buddha. Sunita felt awkward and uncomfortable as Sariputta and the Buddha scrubbed him clean, but he didn't dare protest. The Buddha asked Meghiya to go up and ask Ananda for an extra robe. After Sunita was ordained, the Buddha assigned him to Sariputta's care. Sariputta led him back to Jetavana while the Buddha and the rest of the bhikkhus calmly continued their begging.

The local people had witnessed all of this taking place. News quickly spread that the Buddha had accepted an untouchable into his sangha. This caused a furor among higher castes in the capital. Never in the history of Kosala had an untouchable been accepted into a spiritual community. Many condemned the Buddha for violating sacred tradition. Others went so far as to suggest that the Buddha was plotting to overthrow the existing order and wreak havoc in the country.

The echoes of all these accusations reached the monastery through lay disciples as well as from bhikkhus who heard people saying such things in the city. Senior disciples Sariputta, Mahakassapa, Moggallana, and Anuruddha met to discuss the people's reactions with the Buddha.

The Buddha said, "Accepting untouchables into the sangha was simply a question of time. Our way is a way of equality. We do not recognize caste. Though we may encounter difficulties over Sunita's ordination now, we will have opened a door for the first time in history that future generations will thank us for. We must have courage."

Moggallana said, "We do not lack courage or endurance. But how can we help reduce the hostility of public opinion to make it easier for the bhikkhus to practice?"

Sariputta said, "The important thing is to remain trusting of our practice. I will strive to assist Sunita in making progress on the path. His success will be the strongest argument in our favor. We can also seek ways to explain our belief in equality to the people. What do you think, Master?"

The Buddha placed his hand on Sariputta's shoulder. "You have just spoken my own thoughts," he said.

Before long, the uproar over Sunita's ordination reached the ears of King Pasenadi. A group of religious leaders requested a private audience with him and expressed their grave concerns over the matter. Their convincing arguments disturbed the king, and although he was a devoted follower of the Buddha, he promised the leaders that he would look into the matter. Some days later he paid a visit to Jetavana.

He climbed down from his carriage and walked into the monastery grounds alone. Bhikkhus passed him on the path beneath the cool shade of trees. The king followed the path that led to the Buddha's hut. He bowed to each bhikkhu he passed. As always, the serene and composed manner of the bhikkhus reinforced his faith in the Buddha. Halfway to the hut, he encountered a bhikkhu sitting on a large rock beneath a great pine tree teaching a small group of bhikkhus and lay disciples. It was a most appealing sight. The bhikkhu offering the teaching looked less than forty years old, yet his face radiated great peace and wisdom. His listeners were clearly absorbed by what he had to say. The king paused to listen and was moved by what he heard. But suddenly he remembered the purpose of his visit, and he continued on his way. He hoped to return later to listen to the bhikkhu's teaching.

The Buddha welcomed the king outside his hut, inviting him to sit on a bamboo chair. After they exchanged formal greetings, the king asked the Buddha who the bhikkhu sitting on the rock was. The Buddha smiled and answered, "That is Bhikkhu Sunita. He was once an untouchable who carried night soil. What do you think of his teaching?"

The king felt embarrassed. The bhikkhu with so radiant a bearing was none other than the night soil carrier Sunita! He would never have guessed such was possible. Before he knew how to respond, the Buddha said, "Bhikkhu Sunita has devoted himself wholeheartedly to his practice from the day of his ordination. He is a man of great sincerity, intelligence, and resolve. Though he was ordained only three months ago, he has already earned a reputation for great virtue and purity of heart. Would you like to meet him and make an offering to this most worthy bhikkhu?"

The king replied with frankness, "I would indeed like to meet Bhikkhu Sunita and make an offering to him. Master, your teaching is deep and wondrous! I have never met any other spiritual teacher with so open a heart and mind. I do not think there is a person, animal, or plant that does not benefit from the presence of your understanding. I must tell you that I came here today with the intention of asking how you could accept an untouchable into your sangha. But I have seen, heard, and understood why. I no longer dare ask such a question. Instead, allow me to prostrate myself before you."

The king stood up intending to prostrate himself, but the Buddha stood up, as well, and took the king's hand. He asked the king to be seated again. When they were both seated, the Buddha looked at the king and said, "Majesty, in the Way of Liberation, there is no caste. To the eyes of an enlightened person, all people are equal. Every person's blood is red. Every person's tears are salty. We are all human beings. We must find a way for all people to be able to realize their full dignity and potential. That is why I welcomed Sunita into the sangha of bhikkhus."

The king joined his palms. "I understand now. I also know that the path you have chosen will be filled with obstacles and difficulties. But I know you possess the strength and courage needed to overcome all such obstacles. For my own part, I will do everything in my power to support the true teaching."

The king took his leave of the Buddha and returned to the pine tree in hopes of listening to Bhikkhu Sunita's teaching. But Bhikkhu Sunita and his listeners had disappeared. The king saw no more than a few bhikkhus walking slowly and mindfully down the path.

CHAPTER EIGHTEEN

The Elements Will Recombine

One day Meghiya spoke to the Buddha about Nanda's unhappiness as a monk. Nanda had confided to Meghiya how much he missed his fiancee in Kapilavatthu. Nanda said, "I still remember the day I carried the Buddha's bowl back to Nigrodha Park. As I was leaving, Janapada Kalyani looked into my eyes and said, 'Hurry back. I will be waiting for you.' I can so clearly recall the sheen of her black hair as it brushed her slender shoulders. Her image often arises during my sitting meditation. Every time I see her in my mind, I am filled with longing. I am not happy being a monk."

The next afternoon, the Buddha invited Nanda to go for a walk with him. They left Jetavana and headed toward a distant hamlet located by a lake. They sat on a large boulder that overlooked the crystal clear water. A family of ducks swam by leisurely. Birds sang in the overhanging branches of trees.

The Buddha said, "Some of our brothers have told me that you are not happy living the life of a bhikkhu. Is that true?"

Nanda was silent. After a moment, the Buddha asked, "Do you feel ready to return to Kapilavatthu to prepare to take over the throne?"

Nanda replied hastily, "No, no. I have already told everyone that I do not like politics. I know I don't have the ability to rule a kingdom. I do not wish to become the next king."

"Then why are you unhappy being a bhikkhu?"

Again Nanda was silent.

"Do you miss Kalyani?"

Nanda blushed but he did not speak.

The Buddha said, "Nanda, there are many young women here in Kosala as beautiful as your Kalyani. Do you remember the reception we attended at King Pasenadi's palace? Did you notice any women there as pretty as Kalyani?"

Nanda admitted, "Perhaps there are young women here as pretty as she is. But I care only for Kalyani. In this life there is only one Kalyani."

"Nanda, attachment can be a great barrier to spiritual practice. The physical beauty of a woman fades as surely as the beauty of a rose. You know that all things are impermanent. You must learn to penetrate the impermanent nature of things. Look." The Buddha pointed to an old woman leaning on a cane and hobbling across the bamboo bridge. Her face was covered with wrinkles.

"That old woman was surely once a beauty. Kalyani's beauty will also fade with the years. During that same time your search for enlightenment could bring peace and joy for this life and lives to come. Nanda, look at the two monkeys playing over on that branch. You might not find the female attractive with her long, pointed snout and red bottom, but to the male she is the most beautiful monkey on earth. To him she is unique and he would sacrifice his very life to protect her. Can you see that—"

Nanda interrupted the Buddha. "Please don't say anything more. I understand what you are trying to say. I will devote myself more wholeheartedly to my practice."

The Buddha smiled at his younger brother. "Pay special attention to observing your breath. Meditate on your body, feelings, mental formations, consciousness, and objects of your consciousness. Look deeply in order to see the process of birth, growth, and fading of every phenomenon from your own body, emotions, mind, and objects of your mind. If there is anything you don't understand, come and ask me or Sariputta. Nanda, remember that the happiness liberation brings is true, unconditional happiness. It can never be destroyed. Aspire to that happiness."

The sky was growing dark. The Buddha and Nanda stood and walked back to the monastery.

Jetavana now hosted a strong and stable monastic life. The number of bhikkhus living there had risen to five hundred. The following year the Buddha returned to Vesali for the retreat season. The Licchavi princes had transformed Great Forest into a monastery. They had built a two-story Dharma hall with a roof, which they named Kutagara. A number of smaller buildings were scattered throughout the forest of sal trees. The princes were the sponsors of the retreat season with generous contributions from Ambapali.

Bhikkhus throughout Magadha and as far away as Sakya gathered to spend the retreat season there with the Buddha. They numbered six hundred in all. Lay disciples also traveled to spend the rainy season there in order to receive the Buddha's teaching. They brought daily food offerings and attended all the Dharma talks.

One morning in early autumn just after the retreat came to a close, the Buddha received news that King Suddhodana was on his deathbed in Kapilavatthu. The king had sent Prince Mahanama, his nephew, as a messenger to summon the Buddha in hopes of seeing his son one last time. At Mahanama's special request, the Buddha agreed to travel in the carriage in order to save time. Anuruddha, Nanda, Ananda, and Rahula accompanied him. They left so quickly that even the Licchavi princes and Ambapali were unable to see them off. After the carriage departed, two hundred bhikkhus, including all the former princes of the Sakya clan, began to walk toward Kapilavatthu. They wanted to be with the Buddha at his father's funeral.

The royal family met the Buddha at the palace gates. Mahapajapati led him at once into the king's chambers. The king's face, pale and wan, brightened when he saw the Buddha. The Buddha sat down by the bed and took the king's hand in his own. The king, now eighty-two years old, was thin and frail.

The Buddha said, "Father, please breathe gently and slowly. Smile.

Nothing is more important than your breath at this moment. Nanda, Ananda, Rahula, Anuruddha, and I will breathe together with you."

The king looked at each one of them. He smiled and began to follow his breath. No one dared cry. After a moment, the king looked at the Buddha and said, "I have seen clearly the impermanence of life and how, if a person wants happiness, he should not lose himself in a life of desires. Happiness is obtained by living a life of simplicity and freedom."

Queen Gotami told the Buddha, "These past months, the king has lived very simply. He has truly followed your teaching. Your teaching has transformed the lives of every one of us here."

Still holding the king's hand, the Buddha said, "Father, take a deep look at me, at Nanda, and Rahula. Look at the green leaves on the branches outside your window. Life continues. As life continues, so do you. You will continue to live in me and in Nanda and Rahula, and in all beings. The temporal body arises from the four elements, which dissolve only to endlessly recombine again. Father, don't think that because the body passes away, life and death can bind us. Rahula's body is also your body."

The Buddha motioned to Rahula to come and hold the king's other hand. A lovely smile arose on the face of the dying king. He understood the Buddha's words and he no longer feared death.

The king's advisors and ministers were all present. He motioned for them to approach and in a feeble voice said, "During my reign, I have doubtlessly upset and wronged you. Before I die, I ask your forgiveness."

The advisors and ministers could not hold back their tears. Prince Mahanama knelt by the bed and said, "Your majesty, you have been the most virtuous and just of kings. No one here has any reason to fault you."

Mahanama continued, "I humbly wish to suggest that Prince Nanda now leave monastic life and return to Kapilavatthu to ascend the throne. The people would all be happy to see your own son as king. I pledge to assist and support him with all my being."

Nanda looked at the Buddha as if to plead for rescue. Queen Gotami also looked the Buddha's way. Quietly, the Buddha spoke, "Father,

Ministers, please allow me to share my insight in this matter. Nanda does not yet possess the inclination or ability to serve as a political ruler. He needs more years of spiritual practice to be ready for such a task. Rahula is only fifteen years old and too young to become king. I believe Prince Mahanama is the best qualified to be king. He is a man of great intelligence and talent, as well as a man of compassion and understanding. Furthermore, he has served as the king's chief advisor these past six years. On behalf of the royal family, on behalf of the people, I ask Prince Mahanama to accept this difficult responsibility."

Mahanama joined his palms and protested, "I fear my talent falls far short of what is required of a king. Please, your Majesty, Lord Buddha, and Ministers, choose someone more worthy than myself."

The other ministers voiced their approval of the Buddha's suggestion. The king nodded his approval, as well, and called Mahanama to his side. He took Mahanama's hand and said, "Everyone places his trust in you. The Buddha himself has faith in you. You are my nephew and I would be honored and happy to pass the throne on to you. You will continue our line for a hundred generations."

Mahanama bowed, submitting to the king's wishes.

The king was overjoyed. "Now I can close my eyes in peace. I am happy to have seen the Buddha before I left this world. My heart is now without any cares whatsoever. I have no regrets or bitterness. I hope that the Buddha will rest in Kapilavatthu for a time in order to assist Mahanama in the first days of his reign. Your virtue, Lord Buddha, will assure our country a hundred generations of peace." The king's voice faded to barely a whisper.

The Buddha said, "I will remain here for whatever time is needed to help Mahanama."

The king smiled weakly, but his eyes radiated peace. He closed his eyes and passed from this life. Queen Gotami and Yasodhara began to cry. The ministers sobbed in grief. The Buddha folded the king's hands on his chest and then motioned for everyone to stop crying. He told them to follow their breathing. After several moments, he suggested they meet in the outer chamber to discuss arrangements for the funeral. The funeral took place seven days later. More than a thousand brahmans attended the ceremony. But King Suddhodana's funeral was made unique by the presence of five hundred saffron-robed bhikkhus who represented the Way of the Buddha. In addition to the traditional brahmana prayers and recitations, sutras of the Way were chanted. The bhikkhus chanted the Four Noble Truths, the Sutra on Impermanence, the Sutra on Fire, the Sutra on Dependent Co-arising, and the Three Refuges. They chanted in the tongue of Magadhi, which was spoken by all the peoples east of the Ganga.

The Buddha slowly circled the funeral pyre three times. Before he lit the funeral pyre, he said, "Birth, old age, sickness, and death occur in the life of all persons. We should reflect on birth, old age, sickness, and death every day in order to prevent ourselves from becoming lost in desires, and in order to be able to create a life filled with peace, joy, and contentment. A person who has attained the Way looks on birth, old age, sickness, and death with equanimity. The true nature of all *dharmas* is that there is neither birth nor death; neither production nor destruction; and neither increasing nor decreasing."

Once lit, flames consumed the pyre. The sound of gongs and drums intertwined with chanting. The people of Kapilavatthu attended in great numbers to see the Buddha light the king's funeral pyre.

After Mahanama's coronation, the Buddha remained in Kapilavatthu for three months. One day Mahapajapati Gotami visited him at Nigrodha Park. She offered a number of robes and also requested to be ordained as a nun. She said, "If you will allow women to be ordained, many will benefit. Among our clan, many princes have left home to become your disciples. Many of them had wives. Now their wives desire to study the Dharma as nuns. I want to be ordained myself. It would bring me great joy. This has been my sole desire since the king died."

The Buddha was silent for a long moment before he said, "It is not possible."

Mahapajapati pleaded, "I know this is a difficult issue for you. If you accept women into the sangha you will be met with protest and resistance from society. But I do not believe you are afraid of such reactions."

Again the Buddha was silent. He said, "In Rajagaha, there are also a number of women who want to be ordained, but I don't believe it is the right time yet. Conditions are not yet ripe to accept women in the sangha."

Gotami pleaded three times with him, but his answer remained the same. Deeply disappointed, she departed. When she returned to the palace she told Yasodhara of the Buddha's response.

A few days later, the Buddha returned to Vesali. After his departure, Gotami gathered all the women who wished to be ordained. They included a number of young women who had never been married. All the women belonged to the Sakya clan. She told them, "I know beyond a doubt that in the Way of Awakening, all people are equal. Everyone has the capacity to be enlightened and liberated. The Buddha has said so himself. He has accepted untouchables into the sangha. There is no reason he should not accept women. We are full persons too. We can attain enlightenment and liberation. There is no reason to regard women as inferior.

"I suggest we shave our heads, get rid of our fine clothes and jewels, put on the yellow robes of bhikkhus, and walk barefoot to Vesali where we will ask to be ordained. In this way we will prove to the Buddha and everyone else that we are capable of living simply and practicing the Way. We will walk hundreds of miles and beg for our food. This is the only hope we have to be accepted into the sangha."

All the women agreed with Gotami. They saw in her a true leader. Yasodhara smiled. She had long appreciated Gotami's strong will. Gotami was not one to be stopped by any obstacle, as proved by her years of working on behalf of the poor with Yasodhara. The women agreed on a day to put their plan into action.

Gotami said to Yasodhara, "Gopa, it would be best if you didn't come with us this time. Things may go more smoothly. When we have succeeded, there will be plenty of time for you to follow."

Yasodhara smiled in understanding.

CHAPTER NINETEEN

Opening the Door

Early one morning on his way to the lake to get some water, Ananda met Gotami and fifty other women standing not far from the Buddha's hut. Every woman had shaved her head and was wearing a yellow robe. Their feet were swollen and bloody. At first glance, Ananda thought it was a delegation of monks, but suddenly he recognized Lady Gotami. Hardly able to believe his eyes, he blurted out, "Good heavens, Lady Gotami! Where have you come from? Why are your feet so bloody? Why have you and all the ladies come here like this?"

Gotami answered, "Venerable Ananda, we have shaved our heads and given away all our fine clothes and jewels. We no longer have any possessions in this world. We left Kapilavatthu and have walked for fifteen days, sleeping by the roadside and begging for our food in small villages along the way. We wish to show that we are capable of living like bhikkhus. I beseech you, Ananda. Please speak to the Buddha on our behalf. We wish to be ordained as nuns."

Ananda said, "Wait here. I will speak to the Buddha at once. I promise to do all I can."

Ananda entered the Buddha's hut just as the Buddha was putting on his robe. Nagita, the Buddha's assistant at that time, was also present. Ananda told the Buddha all he had just seen and heard. The Buddha did not say anything.

Ananda then asked, "Lord, is it possible for a woman to attain the

Fruits of Stream Enterer, Once-Returner, Never-Returner, and Arhatship?" The Buddha answered, "Beyond a doubt."

"Then why won't you accept women into the sangha? Lady Gotami nurtured and cared for you from the time you were an infant. She has loved you like a son. Now she has shaved her head and renounced all her possessions. She has walked all the way from Kapilavatthu to prove that women can endure anything that men can. Please have compassion and allow her to be ordained."

The Buddha was silent for a long moment. He then asked Nagita to summon Venerables Sariputta, Moggallana, Anuruddha, Bhaddiya, Kimbila, and Mahakassapa. When they arrived, he discussed the situation with them at length. He explained that it was not discrimination against women which made him hesitant to ordain them. He was unsure how to open the sangha to women without creating harmful conflict both within and outside of the sangha.

After a lengthy exchange of ideas, Sariputta said, "It would be wise to create statutes which define the roles of nuns within the sangha. Such statutes would diminish public opposition which is certain to erupt, since there has been discrimination against women for thousands of years. Please consider the following eight rules:

"First, a nun, or *bhikkhuni*, will always defer to a bhikkhu, even if she is older or has practiced longer than he has.

"Second, all bhikkhunis must spend the retreat season at a center within reach of a center of bhikkhus in order to receive spiritual support and further study.

"Third, twice a month, the bhikkhunis should delegate someone to invite the bhikkhus to decide on a date for *uposatha*, the special day of observance. A bhikkhu should visit the nuns, teach them, and encourage them in their practice.

"Fourth, after the rainy season retreat, nuns must attend the Pavarana ceremony and present an account of their practice, not only before other nuns, but before the monks.

"Fifth, whenever a bhikkhuni breaks a precept, she must confess before both the bhikkhunis and the bhikkhus.

"Sixth, after a period of practice as a novice, a bhikkhuni will take full vows before the communities of both monks and nuns.

"Seventh, a bhikkhuni should not criticize or censure a bhikkhu.

"Eighth, a bhikkhuni will not give Dharma instruction to a community of bhikkhus."

Moggallana laughed. "These eight rules are clearly discriminatory. How can you pretend otherwise?"

Sariputta replied, "The purpose of these rules is to open the door for women to join the sangha. They are not intended to discriminate but to help end discrimination. Don't you see?"

Moggallana nodded, acknowledging the merit of Sariputta's statement.

Bhaddiya said, "These eight rules are necessary. Lady Gotami has commanded much authority. She is the Lord's mother. Without rules such as these, it would be difficult for anyone except the Buddha himself to guide her in her practice."

The Buddha turned to Ananda, "Ananda, please go and tell Lady Mahapajapati that if she is willing to accept these eight special rules, she and the other women may be ordained."

The sun had already climbed high into the sky, but Ananda found Lady Gotami and the other women patiently waiting. After hearing the Eight Rules, Gotami was overjoyed. She replied, "Venerable Ananda, please tell the Buddha that just as a young girl gladly accepts a garland of lotus flowers or roses to adorn her hair after washing it with perfumed water, I happily accept the Eight Rules. I will follow them all my life if I am granted permission to be ordained."

Ananda returned to the Buddha's hut and informed him of Lady Gotami's response.

The other women looked at Gotami with concern in their eyes, but she smiled and reassured them, "Don't worry, my sisters. The important thing is that we have earned the right to be ordained. These Eight Rules will not be barriers to our practice. They are the door by which we may enter the sangha."

All fifty-one women were ordained that same day. Venerable Sariputta arranged for them to live temporarily at Ambapali's mango grove. The Buddha also asked Sariputta to teach the nuns the basic practice. Eight days later, Bhikkhuni Mahapajapati paid a visit to the Buddha. She said, "Lord, please show compassion, and explain how I may best make quick progress on the path of liberation."

The Buddha answered, "Bhikkhuni Mahapajapati, the most important thing is to take hold of your own mind. Practice observing the breath and meditate on the body, feelings, mind, and objects of mind. Practicing like that, each day you will experience a deepening of humility, ease, detachment, peace, and joy. When those qualities arise, you can be sure you are on the correct path, the path of awakening and enlightenment."

Bhikkhuni Mahapajapati wanted to build a convent in Vesali in order to enable the nuns to dwell close to the Buddha and his senior disciples. She also wanted later to return to Kapilavatthu to open a convent in her homeland. She sent a messenger to Yasodhara to announce the good news of the women's ordination. Bhikkhuni Gotami knew that the acceptance of women into the sangha would create an uproar. Bitter opposition would undoubtedly result, and many people would condemn the Buddha and his sangha. She knew the Buddha would have to face many difficulties. She was grateful, and understood that the Eight Rules were temporarily necessary to protect the sangha from harmful conflict. She was sure that later on, once the ordination of women was an established fact, the Eight Rules would no longer be necessary.

The Buddha's community now had four streams—the bhikkhus, bhikkhunis, upasakas (male lay disciples), and upasikas (female lay disciples).

Bhikkhuni Mahapajapati gave careful thought as to how the bhikkhunis should dress. The Buddha accepted all her suggestions. The bhikkhus wore three garments—the *antaravasaka*, or pants; the *uttarasanga*, or inner robe; and the *sanghati*, or outer robe. In addition to these three garments, the bhikkhunis added a cloth wrapped around the chest called a *samkakshika*, and a skirt called a *kusulaka*. In addition to their robes and begging bowl, each monk and nun also had the right to own a fan; a water filter; a needle and thread to mend their robes; a pick to clean their teeth; and a razor to shave their heads twice a month.

CHAPTER TWENTY

The Treasure of Insight

When the thirteenth retreat season ended, the Buddha returned to Savatthi. Svasti and Rahula followed him. Svasti had ordained just a few months before, when he turned twenty-one. His sisters and brother were now old enough to be on their own as a family, and they knew how much Svasti had always wanted to study with the Buddha. It was the first time Svasti had been to Jetavana Monastery. He was delighted to discover how beautiful and inviting a place it was to practice. Jetavana was cool, refreshing, and friendly. Everyone smiled warmly at Svasti. They knew that the Sutra on Tending Water Buffaloes had been inspired by him. Svasti was confident that in so supportive an environment he would make great progress in his practice. He was beginning to understand why the Sangha was as important as the Buddha and the Dharma. Sangha was the community of persons practicing the Way of Awareness. It provided support and guidance. It was necessary to take refuge in the sangha.

Rahula turned twenty years old, and Sariputta performed his ordination ceremony. He was now a fully-ordained bhikkhu, and all the community rejoiced. Venerable Sariputta devoted several days prior to the ordination to give Rahula special teaching. Svasti accompanied him during these sessions and so benefited from Sariputta's teaching as well.

After Rahula's ordination, the Buddha also spent time teaching him different methods of contemplation. Svasti was invited to these sessions, too. The Buddha taught them the contemplation on the six sense organs: eyes, ears, nose, tongue, body, and mind; on the six sense objects: forms, sounds, smells, tastes, tactile objects, and objects of mind; and the six sense consciousnesses: eye consciousness, ear consciousness, nose consciousness, taste consciousness, body consciousness, and mind consciousness. The Buddha showed them how to look deeply into the impermanent nature of these eighteen domains of sense, called the eighteen *dhatus*, which comprised the six sense organs; the six sense objects; and the six sense consciousnesses, or internal objects of sense. Perceptions arose because of contact between a sense organ and a sense object. All the domains of sense depended on each other for existence; they were all impermanent and interdependent. If one could understand that, one could penetrate the truth of the emptiness of self and transcend birth and death.

The Buddha gave Rahula the teaching on the emptiness of self in great detail. He said, "Rahula, among the five *skandhas*—body, feelings, perceptions, mental formations, and consciousness—there is nothing that can be considered to be permanent and nothing that can be called a 'self.' The body is not the self. The body is not something that belongs to the self either. The self cannot be found in the body, and the body cannot be found in the self.

"There are three kinds of views of self. The first is that this body is the self, or these feelings, perceptions, mental formations, or consciousness are the self. This is 'the belief in skandha as self,' and it is the first wrong view. But when one says, 'The skandhas are not the self,' one may fall into the second wrong view and believe that the self is something that exists independently from the skandhas and that the skandhas are its possessions. This second wrong view is called 'skandha is different from the self.' The third wrong view consists in the belief that there is a presence of the self in the skandhas, and there is the presence of the skandhas in the self. This is called 'the belief in the presence of skandhas and self in each other.'

"Rahula, practicing deeply the meditation on the emptiness of the self means looking into the five skandhas in order to see that they are neither self, belonging to self, nor interbeing with self. Once we overcome these three wrong views, we can experience the true nature of 'emptiness of all dharmas.'"

Svasti noticed how a bhikkhu at Jetavana named Thera never spoke to anyone else. He always walked alone. Venerable Thera did not disturb anyone nor did he violate any precepts, and yet it seemed to Svasti that he did not live in genuine harmony with the rest of the community. Once Svasti tried to speak with him, but he walked away without responding. The other bhikkhus nicknamed him "the one who lives alone." Svasti had often heard the Buddha encourage the bhikkhus to avoid idle talk, meditate more, and develop self-sufficiency. But Svasti felt that Venerable Thera was not living the kind of self-sufficiency the Buddha intended. Confused, Svasti decided to ask the Buddha about it.

The next day, during his Dharma talk, the Buddha summoned the elder Thera. He asked him, "Is it true that you prefer to keep to yourself and that you do all things alone, avoiding contact with other bhikkhus?"

The bhikkhu answered, "Yes, Lord, that is true. You have told us to be self-sufficient and to practice being alone."

The Buddha turned to the community and said, "Bhikkhus, I will explain what true self-sufficiency is and what is the better way to live alone. A self-sufficient person is a person who dwells in mindfulness. He is aware of what is going on in the present moment, what is going on in his body, feelings, mind, and objects of mind. He knows how to look deeply at things in the present moment. He does not pursue the past nor lose himself in the future, because the past no longer is and the future has not yet come. Life can only take place in the present moment. If we lose the present moment, we lose life. This is the better way to live alone.

"Bhikkhus, what is meant by 'pursuing the past'? To pursue the past means to lose yourself in thoughts about what you looked like in the past, what your feelings were then, what rank and position you held, what happiness or suffering you experienced then. Giving rise to such thoughts entangles you in the past.

"Bhikkhus, what is meant by 'losing yourself in the future'? To lose yourself in the future means to lose yourself in thoughts about the future. You imagine, hope, fear, or worry about the future, wondering what you will look like, what your feelings will be, whether you will have happiness or suffering. Giving rise to such thoughts entangles you in the future.

"Bhikkhus, return to the present moment in order to be in direct contact with life and to see life deeply. If you cannot make direct contact with life, you cannot see deeply. Mindfulness enables you to return to the present moment. But if you are enslaved by desires and anxieties over what is happening in the present, you will lose your mindfulness and you will not be truly present to life.

"Bhikkhus, one who really knows how to be alone dwells in the present moment, even if he is sitting in the midst of a crowd. If a person sitting alone in the middle of a forest is not mindful, if he is haunted by the past and future, he is not truly alone."

The Buddha then recited a gatha to summarize his teaching:

Do not pursue the past.
Do not lose yourself in the future.
The past no longer is.
The future has not yet come.
Looking deeply at life as it is
in the very here and now,
the practitioner dwells
in stability and freedom.
We must be diligent today.
To wait until tomorrow is too late.
Death comes unexpectedly.
How can we bargain with it?
The sage calls a person who knows
how to dwell in mindfulness

The Buddha's Dharma talk that day was most special.

night and day
'one who knows
the better way to live alone.'

After reading the gatha, the Buddha thanked Thera and invited him to be seated again. The Buddha had neither praised nor criticized Thera, but it was clear that the bhikkhu now had a better grasp of what the Buddha meant by being self-sufficient or being alone.

During the Dharma discussion that took place later that evening, Svasti listened to the senior disciples say how important the Buddha's words had been that morning. Venerable Ananda repeated the Buddha's discourse, including the gatha, word for word. Svasti was always amazed at Ananda's memory. Ananda even spoke with the same stress on words as the Buddha. When Ananda was finished, Mahakaccana stood up and said, "I would like to suggest that we make a formal sutra of the Buddha's teaching this morning. I further suggest that we name it the Bhaddekaratta Sutta, the Sutra on Knowing the Better Way to Live Alone. Every bhikkhu should memorize this sutra and put it into practice."

Mahakassapa stood up and voiced his support for Mahakaccana's idea.

The next morning when the bhikkhus were out begging, they encountered a group of children playing by the rice paddies. The children had caught a crab which one boy held down with his forefinger. With his other hand, he ripped one of the crab's claws off. The other children clapped their hands and squealed. Pleased with their reaction, the boy ripped the other claw off. Then he tore all of the crab's legs off, one by one. He tossed the crab back into the paddy and caught another one.

When the children saw the Buddha and bhikkhus arrive, they bowed their heads and then returned to tormenting the next crab. The Buddha told the children to stop. He said, "Children, if someone ripped off your arm or leg, would it hurt?"

"Yes, Teacher," the children answered.

"Did you know that crabs feel pain just as you do?"

The children did not answer.

The Buddha continued, "The crab eats and drinks just like you. It has parents, brothers, and sisters. When you make it suffer, you make its family suffer as well. Think about what you are doing."

The children appeared sorry for what they had done. Seeing that other villagers had gathered around to see what he and the children were talking about, the Buddha used the occasion to offer a teaching about compassion.

He said, "Every living being deserves to enjoy a sense of security and well-being. We should protect life and bring happiness to others. All living beings, whether large or small; whether two-legged or four-legged; whether swimmers or fliers, have a right to live. We should not harm or kill other living beings. We should protect life.

"Children, just as a mother loves and protects her only child at the risk of her own life, we should open our hearts to protect all living beings. Our love should encompass every living being on, below, within, outside, and around us. Day and night, whether standing or walking, sitting or lying down, we should dwell in that love."

The Buddha asked the children to release the crab they had caught. Then he told everyone, "Meditating on love in this way brings happiness first to the one who practices it. You sleep better and wake up more at ease; you do not have nightmares; you are neither sorrowful nor anxious; and you are protected by everyone and everything around you. Those people and beings you bring into your mind of love and compassion bring you great joy and, slowly, their suffering leaves them."

Svasti knew that the Buddha was committed to sharing the teaching with children. To help with that, he and Rahula organized special classes for children at Jetavana. With the assistance of young laypersons, especially Sudatta's four children, the young people gathered for special teaching once a month. Sudatta's son, Kala, was not very enthusiastic at first about attending. He only did so because he was fond of Svasti. But, little by little, his interest grew. Princess Vajiri, the king's daughter, also lent her support to these classes.

One full moon day, she asked the children to bring flowers to offer to the Buddha. The children arrived with flowers picked from their own gardens and from fields along the way to the monastery. Princess Vajiri brought an armful of lotus flowers she had gathered from the palace's lotus pool. When she and the children went to find the Buddha at his hut, they learned he was in the Dharma hall preparing to give a discourse to both bhikkhus and laypersons. The princess led the children quietly into the hall. All the adults moved to make a pathway for the children. They placed their flowers on the small table in front of the Buddha and then bowed. The Buddha smiled and bowed in return. He invited the children to sit right in front of him.

The Buddha's Dharma talk that day was most special. He waited for the children to be seated quietly, and then he slowly stood up. He picked up one of the lotus flowers and held it up before the community. He did not say anything. Everyone sat perfectly still. The Buddha continued to hold up the flower without saying anything for a long time. People were perplexed and wondered what he meant by doing that. Then the Buddha looked out over the community and smiled.

He said, "I have the eyes of true Dharma, the treasure of wondrous insight, and I have just transmitted it to Mahakassapa."

Everyone turned to look at Venerable Kassapa and saw that he was smiling. His eyes had not wavered from the Buddha and the lotus he held. When the people looked back at the Buddha, they saw that he too was looking at the lotus and smiling.

Though Svasti felt perplexed, he knew that the most important thing was to maintain mindfulness. He began to observe his breath as he looked at the Buddha. The white lotus in the Buddha's hand had newly blossomed. The Buddha held it in a most gentle, noble gesture. His thumb and forefinger held the stem of the flower which trailed the shape of his hand. His hand was as beautiful as the lotus itself, pure and wondrous. Suddenly, Svasti truly saw the pure and noble beauty of the flower. There was nothing to think about. Quite naturally, a smile arose on his face.

The Buddha began to speak. "Friends, this flower is a wondrous reality. As I hold the flower before you, you all have a chance to experience it. Making contact with a flower is to make contact with a wondrous reality. It is making contact with life itself.

"Mahakassapa smiled before anyone else because he was able to make contact with the flower. As long as obstacles remain in your minds, you will not be able to make contact with the flower. Some of you asked yourselves, 'Why is Gautama holding that flower up? What is the meaning of his gesture?' If your minds are occupied with such thoughts, you cannot truly experience the flower.

"Friends, being lost in thoughts is one of the things that prevents us from making true contact with life. If you are ruled by worry, frustration, anxiety, anger, or jealousy, you will lose the chance to make real contact with all the wonders of life.

"Friends, the lotus in my hand is only real to those of you who dwell mindfully in the present moment. If you do not return to the present moment, the flower does not truly exist. There are people who can pass through a forest of sandalwood trees without ever really seeing one tree. Life is filled with suffering, but it also contains many wonders. Be aware in order to see both the suffering and the wonders in life.

"Being in touch with suffering does not mean to become lost, in it. Being in touch with the wonders of life does not mean to lose ourselves in them either. Being in touch is to truly encounter life, to see it deeply. If we directly encounter life, we will understand its interdependent and impermanent nature. Thanks to that, we will no longer lose ourselves in desire, anger, and craving. We will dwell in freedom and liberation."

Svasti felt happy. He was glad he had smiled and understood before the Buddha spoke. Venerable Mahakassapa had smiled first. He was one of Svasti's teachers and a senior disciple who had traveled far on the path. Svasti knew he could not compare himself to Mahakassapa and the other elders like Sariputta, Moggallana, and Assaji. After all, he was still only twenty-four years old!

Angulimala prostrated himself at the Buddha's feet.

CHAPTER TWENTY-ONE

Dwelling in the Present Moment

In the spring of the following year, the Buddha delivered the Satipatthana Sutta, the Sutra on the Four Establishments of Mindfulness, to a gathering of more than three hundred bhikkhus in Kammassadhamma, which was the capital of Kuru. This was a sutra fundamental for the practice of meditation. The Buddha referred to it as the path which could help every person attain peace of body and mind, overcome all sorrows and lamentations, destroy suffering and grief, and attain highest understanding and total emancipation. Later, Venerable Sariputta told the community that this was one of the most important sutras the Buddha had ever given. He encouraged every bhikkhu and bhikkhuni to study, memorize, and practice it.

Venerable Ananda repeated every word of the sutra later that night. Sati means, "to dwell in mindfulness." That is, the practitioner remains aware of everything taking place in his body, feelings, mind, and objects of mind—the four establishments of mindfulness, or awareness.

First the practitioner observes his body—his breath; the four bodily postures of walking, standing, lying, and sitting; bodily actions such as going forward and backward, looking, putting on robes, eating, drinking, using the toilet, speaking, and washing robes; the parts of the body such as hair, teeth, sinews, bones, internal organs, marrow, intestines, saliva, and sweat; the elements which compose the body such as water, air, and heat; and the stages of a body's decay from the time it dies to when the bones turn to dust.

While observing the body, the practitioner is aware of all details concerning the body. For example, while breathing in, the practitioner knows he is breathing in; while breathing out, he knows he is breathing out; breathing in and making his whole body calm and at peace, the practitioner knows he is breathing in and making his whole body calm and at peace. Walking, the practitioner knows he is walking. Sitting, the practitioner knows he is sitting. Performing movements such as putting on robes or drinking water, the practitioner knows he is putting on robes or drinking water. The contemplation of the body is not realized only during the moments of sitting meditation, but throughout the entire day, including the moments one is begging, eating, and washing one's bowl.

In the contemplation of feelings, the practitioner contemplates feelings as they arise, develop, and fade, and feelings, which are pleasant, unpleasant, or neutral. Feelings can have as their source either the body or the mind. When he feels pain from a toothache, the practitioner is aware that he feels pain from a toothache; when he is happy because he has received praise, the practitioner is aware that he is happy because he has received praise. The practitioner looks deeply in order to calm and quiet every feeling in order to clearly see the sources, which give rise to feelings. The contemplation of feelings does not take place only during the moments of sitting meditation. It is practiced throughout the day.

In the contemplation of mind, the practitioner contemplates the presence of his mental states. Craving, he knows he is craving; not craving, he knows he is not craving. Angry or drowsy, he knows he is angry or drowsy; not angry or drowsy, he knows he is not angry or drowsy. Centered or distracted, he knows he is centered or distracted. Whether he is open minded, closed minded, blocked, concentrated, or enlightened, the practitioner knows at once. And if he is not experiencing any of those states, the practitioner also knows at once. The practitioner recognizes, and is aware of, every mental state that arises within him in the present moment.

In the contemplation of the objects of mind, the practitioner contemplates the five hindrances to liberation (sense desire, ill-will, drowsiness, agitation, and doubt); the five skandhas that comprise a person (body, feelings, perceptions, mental formations, and consciousness); the six sense organs and the six sense objects; the Seven Factors of Awakening (full attention, investigating dharmas, energy, joy, ease, concentration, and letting go); and the Four Noble Truths (the existence of suffering, the causes of suffering, liberation from suffering, and the path that leads to liberation from suffering). These are all objects of the mind, and they contain all dharmas.

The Buddha carefully explained each of the four establishments. He said that whoever practiced these four establishments for seven years would attain emancipation. He added that anyone who practiced them for seven months could also attain emancipation. He said that even after practicing these four contemplations for seven days, one could attain emancipation.

During a Dharma discussion, Venerable Assaji reminded the community that this was not the first time the Buddha had taught the Four Establishments of Mindfulness. He had, in fact, spoken about them on several occasions, but this was the first time he had compiled all of his previous teachings on the subject in such a complete and thorough way. Assaji agreed with Sariputta that this sutra should be memorized, recited, and practiced by every bhikkhu and bhikkhuni.

When the Buddha returned to Jetavana toward the end of spring that year, he met and transformed a notorious murderer named Angulimala. One morning when the Buddha entered Savatthi, it seemed like a ghost town. All doors were bolted shut. No one was out in the streets. The Buddha stood in front of a home where he normally received food offerings. The door opened a crack and, seeing it was the Buddha, the owner hastily ran out and invited him to enter. Once inside, the owner latched the door and invited the Buddha to sit. He suggested the Buddha remain inside the house to eat his meal. He said, "Lord, it is very dangerous to go outdoors today. The murderer Angulimala has been seen in these parts. They say he has killed many people in other cities. Every time he kills someone, he cuts off one of their fingers and adds it to a string he wears around his neck. They say that once he has killed a hundred people and has a talisman of a hundred fingers hanging around his neck, he will gain even more terrible, evil powers. It is strange—he never steals anything from the people he murders. King Pasenadi has organized a brigade of soldiers and police to hunt him down."

The Buddha asked, "Why must the king enlist the aid of an entire brigade of soldiers to hunt down just one man?"

"Respected Gautama, Angulimala is very dangerous. He possesses phenomenal fighting skills. Once he overcame forty men who surrounded him on a street. He killed most of them. The survivors had to flee for their lives. Angulimala is said to hide out in Jalini Forest. No one dares pass by there anymore. Not long ago, twenty armed police entered the forest to try to capture him. Only two came out alive. Now that Angulimala has been spotted in the city, no one dares go out to work or shop."

The Buddha thanked the man for telling him about Angulimala and then stood up to take his leave. The man implored the Buddha to remain safely inside, but the Buddha refused. He said that he could only preserve the trust of the people by continuing to do his begging as usual.

As the Buddha walked slowly and mindfully down the street, he suddenly heard the sound of steps running behind him in the distance. He knew it was Angulimala, but he felt no fear. He continued to take slow steps, aware of everything taking place within and outside of himself.

Angulimala shouted, "Stop, monk! Stop!"

The Buddha continued taking slow, stable steps. He knew from the sound of Angulimala's footsteps that he had slowed down to a brisk walk and was not far behind. Although the Buddha was now fifty-six years old, his sight and hearing were keener than ever. He held nothing but his begging bowl. He smiled as he recollected how quick and agile he had been in martial arts as a young prince. The other young men were never able to deliver him a blow. The Buddha knew that Angulimala was very close now and was surely carrying a weapon.

The Buddha continued to walk with ease.

When Angulimala caught up to the Buddha, he walked alongside him and said, "I told you to stop, monk. Why don't you stop?"

The Buddha continued to walk as he said, "Angulimala, I stopped a long time ago. It is you who have not stopped."

Angulimala was startled by the Buddha's unusual reply. He blocked the Buddha's path, forcing the Buddha to stop. The Buddha looked into Angulimala's eyes. Again, Angulimala was startled. The Buddha's eyes shone like two stars. Angulimala had never encountered someone who radiated such serenity and ease. Everyone else always ran away from him in terror. Why didn't this monk show any fear? The Buddha was looking at him as if he were a friend or brother. The Buddha had said Angulimala's name, so it was clear that he knew who Angulimala was. Surely he knew about his treacherous deeds. How could he remain so calm and relaxed when faced with a murderer? Suddenly Angulimala felt he could no longer bear the Buddha's kind and gentle gaze. He said, "Monk, you said you stopped a long time ago. But you were still walking. You said I was the one who has not stopped. What did you mean by that?"

The Buddha replied, "Angulimala, I stopped committing acts that cause suffering to other living beings a long time ago. I have learned to protect life, the lives of all beings, not just humans. Angulimala, all living beings want to live. All fear death. We must nurture a heart of compassion and protect the lives of all beings."

"Human beings do not love each other. Why should I love other people? Humans are cruel and deceptive. I will not rest until I have killed them all."

The Buddha spoke gently, "Angulimala, I know you have suffered deeply at the hands of other humans. Sometimes humans can be most cruel. Such cruelty is the result of ignorance, hatred, desire, and jealousy. But humans can also be understanding and compassionate. Have you ever met a bhikkhu before? Bhikkhus vow to protect the lives of all other beings. They vow to overcome desire, hatred, and ignorance. There are many people, not just bhikkhus, whose lives are based on understanding and love. Angulimala, there may be cruel people in this world, but there are also many kind people. Do not be blinded. My path can transform cruelty into kindness. Hatred is the path you are on now. You should stop. Choose the path of forgiveness, understanding, and love instead."

Angulimala was moved by the monk's words, yet his mind was thrown into confusion. Suddenly, he felt as if he had been cut open and salt had been thrown on the open wound. He could see that the Buddha spoke from love. There was no hatred in the Buddha, no aversion. The monk looked at Angulimala as if he considered him a whole person, worthy of respect. Could this monk be the very Gautama he had heard people praise, the one they called "the Buddha"? Angulimala asked, "Are you the monk Gautama?" The Buddha nodded.

Angulimala said, "It is a great pity I did not meet you sooner. I have gone too far already on my path of destruction. It is no longer possible to turn back."

The Buddha said, "No, Angulimala, it is never too late to do a good act."

"What good act could I possibly do?"

"Stop traveling the road of hatred and violence. That would be the greatest act of all. Angulimala, though the sea of suffering is immense, look back and you will see the shore."

"Gautama, even if I wanted to, I could not turn back now. No one would let me live in peace after all I have done."

The Buddha grasped Angulimala's hand and said, "Angulimala, I will protect you if you vow to abandon your mind of hatred and devote yourself to the study and practice of the Way. Take the vow to begin anew and serve others. It is easy to see you are a man of intelligence. I have no doubt you could succeed on the path of realization."

Angulimala knelt before the Buddha. He removed the sword strapped to his back, placed it on the earth, and prostrated himself at the Buddha's feet. He covered his face in his hands and began to sob. After a long time, he looked up and said, "I vow to abandon my evil ways. I will follow you and learn compassion from you. I beg you to accept me as your disciple."

At that moment, Venerables Sariputta, Ananda, Upali, Kimbila, and several other bhikkhus arrived on the scene. They surrounded the Buddha and Angulimala. Seeing the Buddha safe and Angulimala preparing to take the refuges, their hearts rejoiced. The Buddha asked Ananda to give him an extra set of robes. He told Sariputta to ask the next house if they could borrow a razor for Upali to shave Angulimala's head. Angulimala was ordained right then and there. He knelt down, recited the three refuges, and was given the precepts by Upali. Afterward, they returned to Jetavana together.

Over the next ten days, Upali and Sariputta taught Angulimala about the practice of the precepts, the practice of meditation, and the way of begging. Angulimala made a greater effort than any other bhikkhu before him. Even the Buddha was astonished at his transformation when he visited Angulimala two weeks after his ordination. Angulimala radiated serenity and stability, and so rare a gentleness that the other bhikkhus called him "Ahimsaka" which means "Nonviolent One." It had, in fact, been his name at birth. Svasti found it a most fitting name for him for, outside of the Buddha, there was no other bhikkhu whose gaze was more filled with kindness.

One morning, the Buddha entered Savatthi to beg, accompanied by fifty other bhikkhus, including bhikkhu Ahimsaka. As they reached the city gates, they met King Pasenadi mounted on a steed, leading a battalion of soldiers. The king and his generals were dressed in full fighting gear. When the king saw the Buddha, he dismounted and bowed.

The Buddha asked, "Majesty, has something happened? Has another kingdom invaded your borders?"

The king replied, "Lord, no one has invaded Kosala. I have gathered these soldiers to capture the murderer Angulimala. He is extremely dangerous. No one has yet been able to bring him to justice. He was seen in the city just two weeks ago. My people are still living in constant fear."

The Buddha asked, "Are you sure Angulimala is really that dangerous?"

The king said, "Lord, Angulimala is a danger to every man, woman, and child. I cannot rest until he is found and killed."

The Buddha asked, "If Angulimala repented his ways and vowed never to kill again, if he took the vows of a bhikkhu and respected all living beings, would you still need to capture and kill him?"

"Lord, if Angulimala became your disciple and followed the precept against killing, if he lived the pure and harmless life of a bhikkhu, my happiness would know no bounds! Not only would I spare his life and grant him freedom, I would offer him robes, food, and medicine. But I hardly think such a thing will come to pass!"

The Buddha pointed to Ahimsaka standing behind him and said, "Your majesty, this monk is none other than Angulimala. He has taken the precepts of a bhikkhu. He has become a new man in these past two weeks."

King Pasenadi was horrified when he realized he was standing so close to the notorious killer.

The Buddha said, "There is no need to fear him, your majesty. Bhikkhu Angulimala is gentler than a handful of earth. We call him Ahimsaka now."

The king stared long and hard at Ahimsaka and then bowed to him. He asked, "Respected monk, what family were you born into? What was your father's name?"

"Your majesty, my father's name was Gagga. My mother was Mantani."

"Bhikkhu Gagga Mantaniputta, allow me to offer you robes, food, and medicine."

Ahimsaka answered, "Thank you, your majesty, but I have three robes already. I receive my food each day by begging, and I have no need for medicine at present. Please accept my heartfelt gratitude for your offer."

The king bowed again to the new bhikkhu and then turned to the Buddha. "Enlightened Master, your virtue is truly wondrous! You bring peace and well-being to situations no one else can. What others fail to resolve by force and violence, you resolve by your great virtue. Let me express my profound gratitude."

The king departed after informing his generals they could disband the troops, and everyone could return to their regular duties.

CHAPTER TWENTY-TWO

The Raft is Not the Shore

That winter the Buddha stayed in Vesali. One day while he was meditating not far from Kutagarasala Dharma Hall, several bhikkhus committed suicide in another part of the monastery. When the Buddha was informed, he asked what led them to kill themselves. He was told that after meditating on the impermanent and fading nature of the body, these bhikkhus expressed aversion for the body and no longer wished to live. The Buddha was saddened to hear this. He called all the remaining bhikkhus together.

He said, "Bhikkhus, we meditate on impermanence and fading in order to see into the true nature of all dharmas so that we will not be bound by them. Enlightenment and freedom cannot be attained by escaping the world. They can only be attained when one sees deeply into the true nature of all dharmas. These brothers did not understand and so they foolishly sought to escape. By doing so, they violated the precept against killing.

"Bhikkhus, a liberated person neither clings to dharmas nor feels aversion to them. Clinging and aversion are both ropes that bind. A free person transcends both in order to dwell in peace and happiness. Such happiness cannot be measured. A free person does not cling to narrow views about permanence and a separate self, nor does he cling to narrow views about impermanence and non-self. Bhikkhus, study and practice the teaching intelligently in a spirit of non-attachment." And the Buddha taught the bhikkhus the practice of conscious breathing to help them refresh themselves.

When he returned to Savatthi, the Buddha gave further teaching on breaking through attachment in response to a bhikkhu named Arittha, who was bound to narrow views because he also misunderstood the teaching. Sitting before the bhikkhus at Jetavana, the Buddha said, "Bhikkhus, if the teaching is misunderstood, it is possible to become caught in narrow views which will create suffering for oneself and others. You must listen to, understand, and apply the teaching in an intelligent manner. Someone who understands snakes uses a forked stick to pin down a snake's neck before trying to pick it up. If he picks the snake up by the tail or body, the snake can easily bite him. Just as you would use your intelligence in catching a snake, you should use it to study the teaching.

"Bhikkhus, the teaching is merely a vehicle to describe the truth. Don't mistake it for the truth itself. A finger pointing at the moon is not the moon. The finger is needed to know where to look for the moon, but if you mistake the finger for the moon itself, you will never know the real moon.

"The teaching is like a raft that carries you to the other shore. The raft is needed, but the raft is not the other shore. An intelligent person would not carry the raft around on his head after making it across to the other shore. Bhikkhus, my teaching is the raft, which can help you cross to the other shore beyond birth and death. Use the raft to cross to the other shore, but don't hang on to it as your property. Do not become caught in the teaching. You must be able to let it go.

"Bhikkhus, all the teachings I have given you, such as the Four Noble Truths, the Noble Eightfold Path, the Four Establishments of Mindfulness, the Seven Factors of Awakening, Impermanence, Nonself, Suffering, Emptiness, Signlessness, and Aimlessness, should be studied in an intelligent, open manner. Use the teachings to help you reach liberation. Do not become attached to them."

The monastery for bhikkhunis housed five hundred nuns. They

frequently invited the Buddha and other Venerables from Jetavana to come and give them Dharma talks. Venerable Ananda was asked by the Buddha to be in charge of selecting which monks should go to deliver Dharma talks to the bhikkhunis. One day he assigned Venerable Bhanda to go. Venerable Bhanda had attained deep fruits in his practice, but he was not noted for his speaking talent. The following day, after begging and eating his meal alone in the forest, he went to the bhikkhunis' center. The sisters warmly received him and Bhikkhuni Gotami invited him to sit on the pedestal to give his Dharma talk.

After settling on his cushion, he recited a short poem:

> Dwelling in tranquility,
> seeing the Dharma, returning to the source
> without hatred or violence,
> joy and peace overflow.
> Mindfulness is held perfectly;
> true peace and ease are realized.
> Transcending all desires
> is the greatest happiness.

The Venerable said no more, but proceeded to enter into a state of deep concentration. Though his words had been few, his presence radiated peace and happiness, which most of the sisters found greatly encouraging. Some of the younger sisters, however, were disappointed by how short his talk was. They urged Bhikkhuni Gotami to ask if he might say something more. Bhikkhuni Gotami bowed to Venerable Bhanda and expressed the wish of the younger sisters. But Venerable Bhanda simply repeated the same poem again and then stepped down from the pedestal.

Some days later, the Buddha was told about Venerable Bhanda's Dharma talk. It was suggested to the Buddha that, in the future, monks more talented at speaking should give the Dharma talks. But the Buddha replied that a person's presence was more important than his words.

One morning, after returning from his begging, the Buddha was unable to find Ananda. Venerable Rahula and others said they had

Prakriti offered Ananda a drink of water from the well.

not seen him. Then one bhikkhu reported that he had seen Ananda go begging in a nearby village of untouchables. The Buddha asked that bhikkhu to go to the village and look for Ananda. The bhikkhu found Ananda and returned with him to the monastery. He also brought back two women, a mother, and her daughter, whose name was Prakriti.

The Buddha listened to Ananda explain how he had been delayed that day. One day, several weeks before, on his way back to the monastery after begging, Ananda suddenly felt thirsty. He stopped by the well in the untouchable village for a drink. There he found Prakriti lifting a bucket of water from the well. She was a beautiful young woman. Ananda asked her for a drink of water, but she refused. She told him she was an untouchable and did not dare pollute a monk by offering him water.

Ananda told her, "I do not need high rank or caste. I only need a drink of water. I would be happy to receive it from you. Please don't be afraid of polluting me."

Prakriti offered him water at once. She felt drawn to this kind and handsome monk who spoke so gently. She was smitten with love. At night she could not sleep. All her thoughts were of Ananda. She waited by the well every day after that in hopes of catching a glimpse of him. She persuaded her mother to invite him to share a meal in their home. He accepted twice, but sensing that the young woman had fallen in love with him, he refused additional invitations.

Prakriti was lovesick. She grew thin and pale. Finally she confessed her feelings to her mother. She said she wanted Ananda to renounce his vows and marry her. Her shocked mother shouted at her and told her it was a foolish and impossible love. But Prakriti said she would sooner die than give up Ananda. Fearing for her daughter's health, Prakriti's mother prepared an aphrodisiac in hopes she might get Ananda to respond to her daughter's passion. She was from the Matanga clan and knew a number of shamanistic potions.

That morning, Prakriti met Ananda on the street and implored him to accept one last invitation to eat at their home. Ananda was confident he could offer Prakriti and her mother teaching that would enable Prakriti to let go of her desire for him. But he had no chance to teach anything before he drank the tainted tea. His head began to swim and his limbs went weak. He realized at once what had happened, and he turned to his breathing to counteract the effects of the herbs. The bhikkhu sent by the Buddha found him in Prakriti's hut, sitting perfectly still in the lotus position.

The Buddha gently asked Prakriti, "You love Bhikkhu Ananda deeply, don't you?"

Prakriti answered, "I love him with all my heart."

"What is it you love about him? Is it his eyes, his nose, or perhaps his mouth?"

"I love everything about him—his eyes, his nose, his mouth, his voice, the way he walks. Master, I love everything about him."

"Besides his eyes, nose, mouth, voice, and walk, Bhikkhu Ananda possesses many beautiful qualities which you do not know yet."

"What qualities are those?" asked Prakriti.

The Buddha answered, "His heart of love is one. Do you know what Bhikkhu Ananda loves?"

"Sir, I do not know what he loves. I only know that he doesn't love me."

"You are mistaken. Bhikkhu Ananda does love you, but not in the way you desire. Bhikkhu Ananda loves the path of liberation, freedom, peace, and joy. Thanks to the liberation and freedom he experiences, Bhikkhu Ananda often smiles. He loves all other beings. He wants to bring the path of liberation to all others so that they too may enjoy freedom, peace, and joy. Prakriti, Bhikkhu Ananda's love comes from understanding and liberation. He does not suffer or feel hopeless because of his love, unlike the way your love makes you feel. If you truly love Bhikkhu Ananda, you will understand his love and you will allow him to continue living the life of liberation he has chosen. If you knew how to love in the way Bhikkhu Ananda does, you would no longer suffer and feel hopeless. Your suffering and hopelessness result from your wanting Bhikkhu Ananda all to yourself. That is a selfish kind of love."

Prakriti looked at the Buddha and asked, "But how can I love in the way that Bhikkhu Ananda loves?"

"Love in a way that will preserve the happiness of Bhikkhu Ananda as well as your own happiness. Bhikkhu Ananda is like a fresh breeze. If you catch a breeze and trap it in a prison of love, the breeze will soon die, and no one will be able to benefit from its coolness, including yourself. Love Ananda as you would a refreshing breeze. Prakriti, if you could love like that, you could become a cool, refreshing breeze yourself. You would relieve your own pains and burdens and those of many others as well."

"Please, Master, teach me how to love in such a way."

"You can choose the same path as Bhikkhu Ananda. You can live a life of liberation, peace, and joy, bringing happiness to others just as Bhikkhu Ananda does. You could be ordained just as he is."

"But I am an untouchable! How can I be ordained?"

"We have no caste in our sangha. Several untouchable men have already been ordained as bhikkhus. Venerable Sunita, so highly regarded by King Pasenadi, was an untouchable. If you wanted to become a bhikkhuni, you would be the first nun to come from the untouchables. If you want, I will ask Sister Khema to perform an ordination ceremony for you."

Overcome with joy, Prakriti prostrated herself before the Buddha and asked to be ordained. The Buddha gave Prakriti into Sister Khema's care. After the nun and young woman departed, the Buddha looked at Ananda and then spoke to the entire community.

"Bhikkhus, Ananda's vows are still intact, but I want all of you to be more careful in your outside relations. If you dwell continuously in mindfulness, you will see what is taking place both within and without you. Detecting something early on will enable you to deal effectively with it. By practicing mindfulness every moment of your daily life, you will be able to develop the concentration needed to avoid situations such as this. When your concentration is strong and stable, your vision will be clear and your actions timely. Concentration and understanding go hand in hand with each other; each contains the other. They are one.

"Bhikkhus, regard women older than yourself as your mother or elder sister. Regard women younger than yourself as your younger sister or daughter. Do not let your attractions create difficulties for your practice. If necessary, until your concentration is stronger, omit your contacts with women. Speak only words which relate to the study and practice of the Way."

The bhikkhus were happy to receive the Buddha's guidance.

CHAPTER TWENTY-THREE

All the Way to the Sea

During his travels, the Buddha stopped in the village of Alavi. The Buddha and eight bhikkhus were offered a meal in a public building there, while all the local people were served food as well. Following the meal, the Buddha was about to begin a Dharma talk when an elderly farmer, almost out of breath, entered the hall. He was late because he'd had to search for a lost water buffalo. The Buddha could see that the old farmer had not eaten all day, and he asked that rice and curry be served to the old man before he would begin the Dharma talk. Many people felt impatient. They did not understand why one man should be allowed to hold up the Buddha's discourse.

When the farmer had finished eating, the Buddha said, "Respected friends, if I delivered a Dharma talk while our brother was still hungry, he would not be able to concentrate. That would be a pity. There is no greater suffering than hunger. Hunger wastes our bodies and destroys our well-being, peace, and joy. We should never forget those who are hungry. It is a discomfort to miss one meal, but think of the suffering of those who have not had a proper meal in days, or even weeks. We must find ways to assure that no one in this world is forced to go hungry."

After Alavi, the Buddha followed the Ganga northwest toward Kosambi. He paused to watch a piece of driftwood being carried downstream. He called to the other bhikkhus, pointed to the piece of wood, and said, "Bhikkhus! If that piece of driftwood does not become lodged against the riverbank; if it does not sink; if it does not become moored on a sandbar; if it isn't lifted out of the water; if it isn't caught in a whirlpool; or if it doesn't rot from the inside out, it will float all the way to the sea. It is the same for you on the path. If you don't become lodged against the riverbank; if you don't sink; if you don't become moored on a sandbar; if you are not lifted out of the water; if you do not become caught in a whirlpool; or if you don't rot from the inside out, you are certain to reach the great sea of enlightenment and emancipation."

The bhikkhus said, "Please, Lord, explain this more fully. What does it mean to become lodged against the riverbank, to sink, or to be moored on a sandbar?"

The Buddha answered, "To become lodged against the riverbank is to become entangled by the six senses and their objects. If you practice diligently, you will not become entangled in feelings, which result from contact between the senses and their objects. To sink means to become enslaved by desire and greed, which rob you of the strength needed to persevere in your practice. To become moored on a sandbar means to worry about serving only your own desires, forever seeking advantages and prestige for yourself while forgetting the goal of enlightenment. To be lifted from the water means to lose yourself in dispersion, loitering with people of poor character instead of pursuing the practice. To be caught in a whirlpool means to be bound by the five categories of desire—being caught by good food, sex, money, fame, or sleep. To rot from the inside out means to live a life of false virtue, deceiving the sangha while using the Dharma to serve your own desires.

"Bhikkhus, if you practice diligently and avoid these six traps, you will certainly attain the fruit of enlightenment, just as that piece of driftwood will make it to the sea if it overcomes all obstacles."

As the Buddha spoke these words to the bhikkhus, a youth tending water buffaloes nearby stopped to listen. His name was Nanda. He was so moved by the Buddha's words, that he approached the bhikkhus and asked to be accepted as a disciple. He said, "Teacher, I want to be a bhikkhu like these brothers. I want to follow the spiritual path. I promise to devote myself to studying the Way. I will avoid becoming caught against the riverbank, sinking, becoming moored on a sandbar, being lifted from the water, becoming caught in a whirlpool, and rotting from the inside out. Please accept me as a disciple."

The Buddha was pleased by the young man's bright countenance. He knew the young man was capable and diligent, although he had probably had little or no schooling. The Buddha nodded his acceptance and asked, "How old are you?"

Nanda answered, "Master, I am sixteen."

"Are your parents living?"

"No, Master, they are both dead. I have no other family. I take care of a rich man's water buffaloes in exchange for shelter."

The Buddha asked, "Can you live on just one meal a day?"

"I have been doing that already for a long time."

The Buddha said, "In principle, you should be twenty years old before being accepted into the sangha. Most young men are not mature enough to live the life of a homeless monk until they are at least twenty. But you are clearly special. I will ask the community to waive the usual requirement in your case. You can practice as a *samanera* novice for four years before taking the full precepts. Return the water buffaloes and ask your master's permission to leave his employment. We will wait here for you."

The youth replied, "Master, I do not think that will be necessary. These buffaloes are very obedient. They will return to the stable on their own even without my assistance."

The Buddha said, "No, you must lead them back yourself and speak to your master before you can join us."

"But what if you are gone by the time I return?"

The Buddha smiled. "Do not worry. You have my word that we will wait here for you."

While Nanda led the buffaloes back to their stable, the Buddha spoke with Svasti. "Svasti, I will place this young man under your care. I

Bhikkhu Rahula took off his robe so that
he could ride on the back of the water buffalo.

believe you understand best how to guide and support him."

Svasti joined his palms and smiled. Venerable Svasti was thirty-nine years old now. He knew why the Buddha wanted him to be young Nanda's instructor. Long ago, the Buddha delivered the Sutra on Tending Water Buffaloes after being inspired by his friendship with Svasti when Svasti was a buffalo boy like Nanda. Svasti knew he could guide Nanda well on the path. He knew that his closest friend, Venerable Rahula, would assist him also. Rahula was now thirty-six.

Svasti's siblings were all grown with families of their own. The hut they once shared had long since perished. Svasti recalled with a smile the visit he made to Uruvela one year with Rahula.

It was after his brother Rupak had married and moved to another village. At that time his sisters Bhima and Bala still lived together and supported themselves by making and selling cakes. Bhikkhus Svasti and Rahula walked to the Neranjara River. Svasti had not forgotten his promise to give Rahula the experience of riding on a water buffalo, and so he called to some young buffalo boys who were grazing their buffaloes near the riverbanks. He asked them to help Bhikkhu Rahula climb onto the back of one of the great beasts. At first Rahula hesitated, but then he removed his sanghati and handed it to Svasti. Rahula was touched by how gentle the mighty beast was. He shared his impressions of the leisurely ride with Svasti, and he wondered aloud what the Buddha would think if he could see him. Svasti smiled. He knew that if Rahula had remained in the Sakya palace to one day become king, he would never have enjoyed this water buffalo ride.

Svasti returned to the present moment just as young Nanda arrived. That night he shaved Nanda's hair and showed him how to wear the robe, carry the begging bowl, walk, stand, lie down, and sit as a mindful bhikkhu. Nanda was mature and diligent, and Svasti enjoyed helping him.

He recalled how some years ago, seventeen young people had been accepted into the sangha at Bamboo Forest. The oldest boy, Upali, was seventeen and the youngest only twelve. They were all from wealthy families. When Upali asked his parents to allow him to become a bhikkhu and they agreed, sixteen of his friends implored their parents to let them do the same. Once they joined the sangha, they were expected to follow the life of a bhikkhu, including eating only one meal before noon. The first night, several of the youngest boys cried from hunger. When the Buddha asked the next morning why he had heard children crying in the night, he was told about the boys being accepted into the community. The Buddha said, "Henceforth, we will accept only young men who are at least twenty years of age into the sangha. Children cannot be expected to live the life of a homeless monk."

The boys were allowed to stay, but the Buddha asked that those fifteen years old and younger be given an additional meal in the evening. All the boys remained bhikkhus. The youngest one, Svasti realized, was already twenty now.

CHAPTER TWENTY-FOUR

Three Wondrous Gates

In the spring the Buddha returned east, stopping at Vesali and Campa. He followed the river to the sea where he taught along the coast. After leaving the coast, the Buddha visited Pataliputta and Vesali, and then headed towards his homeland. Upon reaching the town of Samagama in Sakya, he learned that Nathaputta, leader of the Nigantha sect, had died and that his followers had divided into two bitter camps. Each side denounced the other for false interpretation of doctrine, and each vied for the laity's support. The people were dismayed and confused, and did not know which side to follow.

The novice Cunda, Sariputta's attendant, explained the Nigantha dispute to Ananda. He was aware of all the details because he had lived for a time in Pava where Nathaputta taught. Ananda told the Buddha about the conflict, and then added in a worried tone of voice, "Lord, I hope there will be no split in the sangha after you pass away."

The Buddha patted Ananda on the shoulder and said, "Ananda, do any of the bhikkhus presently argue over the contents of the teaching? Do they argue about the Four Establishments of Mindfulness, the Four Right Efforts, the Five Faculties, the Five Powers, the Seven Factors of Awakening, or the Noble Eightfold Path?"

"No, I have never seen any bhikkhus arguing with each other over the teaching. But you are still among us. We take refuge in your virtue. We all listen to you and our studies proceed peacefully. But when you are gone, disagreements may arise over the precepts, how best to organize the sangha, or how to spread the teaching. If conflicts erupt, many could grow disheartened and even lose their faith in the path."

The Buddha consoled him. "Don't worry, Ananda. If arguments and conflicts arise in the sangha over the contents of the teaching such as the Four Establishments of Mindfulness, the Four Right Efforts, the Five Faculties, the Five Powers, the Seven Factors of Awakening, or the Noble Eightfold Path—that would be cause for worry. Disagreements over small matters concerning the practice of the precepts, sangha organization, and dissemination of the teaching are not worth worrying about."

Despite the Buddha's reassurances, Venerable Ananda remained unconvinced. Only recently he had learned that in Vesali, Venerable Sunakkhata, who had once been the Buddha's attendant, had abandoned the sangha out of personal dissatisfaction. He was organizing lectures at which he denounced the Buddha and the sangha. He exclaimed that the monk Gautama was no more than an ordinary man who possessed no special insight. He said that Gautama's teaching only spoke about liberating one's own self and showed no concern for society as a whole. Sunakkhata was sowing seeds of confusion. Venerable Sariputta was also aware of the situation and shared Ananda's concern.

Ananda knew that seeds of discontent were also being sown in Rajagaha. Several bhikkhus, under the leadership of Venerable Devadatta, were secretly trying to organize a new sangha, independent from the Buddha. Several capable bhikkhus were cooperating with Devadatta, including Venerables Kokalika, Katamoraka Tissa, Khandadeviputta, and Samuddadatta. Devadatta was one of the Buddha's brightest senior disciples. Brother Sariputta had often praised him before the people and had treated him as a special friend. Ananda could not understand why Devadatta had recently grown so jealous of others, especially the Buddha himself. Ananda knew that no one had disclosed these things to the Buddha yet. He was afraid he himself would have to be the one to inform the Buddha of these sad developments before long.

The next year, the Buddha returned to Savatthi for the rainy season.

He dwelled at Jetavana. There he delivered the Sutra on the Dharma Seal. "There is a wonderful teaching which I will speak to you about today. Please empty your minds of all other thoughts in order to calmly and peacefully hear, receive, and understand this teaching.

"Bhikkhus, certain Dharma seals are the signs of true Dharma. There are three seals which every teaching of mine bears. These are Emptiness, Signlessness, and Aimlessness. These three characteristics are the three gates which lead to emancipation. These Dharma seals are also known as the Three Gates of Emancipation, or the Three Liberation Gates.

"Bhikkhus, the first seal is Emptiness, *sunnata*. Emptiness does not mean non-existence. It means that nothing exists independently. Emptiness means empty of a separate self. As you know, the belief in being and the belief in non-being are both incorrect. All dharmas depend on each other for their existence. This is because that is; this is not because that is not; this is born because that is born; this dies because that dies. Thus, the nature of emptiness is interdependence.

"Bhikkhus, practice looking at the interdependent relationships of all dharmas in order to see how all dharmas are present in each other, how one dharma contains all other dharmas. Apart from one dharma, no other dharmas can exist. Contemplate the eighteen realms of the six sense organs, the six sense objects, and the six sense consciousnesses. Contemplate the five aggregates of body, feelings, perceptions, mental formations, and consciousness. You will see that no phenomenon, no aggregate, can exist independently. All depend on each other for existence. When you see this, you will see into the empty nature of all dharmas. Once you see the empty nature of all dharmas, you will no longer chase after or run away from any dharma. You will transcend attachment, discrimination, and prejudice toward all dharmas.

Contemplation on the nature of emptiness opens the first gate to freedom. Emptiness is the first Liberation Gate.

"Bhikkhus, the second seal is Signlessness, *animitta*. Signlessness means to transcend the confines of perception and mental discrimination. When people are unable to see the interdependent and empty nature of all dharmas, they perceive dharmas as being separate and independent phenomena. This exists apart from that; this is independent of all other dharmas. Looking at dharmas in such a way is like taking a sword of mental discrimination and cutting up reality into small pieces. One is then prevented from seeing the true face of reality. Bhikkhus, all dharmas depend on each other. This is in that; this fits within that; and in the one are found the all. That is the meaning of the terms interpenetration and interbeing. This is in that; that is in this. This is that; that is this. Contemplate in this way and you will see that ordinary perception is full of error. The eyes of perception are unable to see as clearly and accurately as the eyes of understanding. The eyes of perception can mistake a rope for a snake. With the illuminating eyes of understanding, the true form of the rope reveals itself and the image of a snake disappears.

"Bhikkhus, all mental concepts such as existence, non-existence, birth, death, one, many, appearing, disappearing, coming, going, defiled, immaculate, increasing, and decreasing are created by perception and mental discrimination. From the view of the unconditioned absolute, the true face of reality cannot be confined within the prisons of such concepts. Thus all dharmas are said to be signless. Contemplate in order to dissolve all thoughts about existence, non-existence, birth, death, one, many, appearing, disappearing, coming, going, defiled, immaculate, increasing, and decreasing, and you will attain liberation. Signlessness is the second Liberation Gate.

"Bhikkhus, the third seal is Aimlessness, *appanihita*. Aimlessness means not chasing after anything. Why? Usually people try to avoid one dharma by chasing after another one. People pursue wealth in order to avoid poverty. The spiritual seeker rejects birth and death in order to attain liberation.

But if all dharmas are contained within each other, if all dharmas are each other, how can you run away from one dharma to pursue a different one? Within birth and death lies *nirvana*; within nirvana lies birth and death. Nirvana and birth and death are not two separate realities. If you reject birth and death in order to pursue nirvana, you have not yet grasped the interdependent nature of all dharmas. You have not yet grasped the empty and formless nature of all dharmas. Contemplate aimlessness in order to end once and for all your chasing and running away.

"Liberation and enlightenment do not exist outside of your own self. We need only open our eyes to see that we ourselves are the very essence of liberation and enlightenment. All dharmas, all beings, contain the nature of full enlightenment within themselves. Don't look for it outside yourself. If you shine the light of awareness on your own self, you will realize enlightenment immediately. Bhikkhus, nothing in the universe exists independently of your own consciousness, not even nirvana or liberation. Don't search for them elsewhere. Remember that the object of consciousness cannot exist independently from consciousness. Don't chase after any dharma, including Brahma, nirvana, and liberation. That is the meaning of aimlessness. You already are what you are searching for. Aimlessness is a wondrous gate that leads to freedom. It is called the third Liberation Gate.

"Bhikkhus, this is the teaching of the Dharma Seals, the teaching of the Three Gates of Emancipation. The Three Gates of Emancipation are wondrous and sublime. Devote yourselves wholeheartedly to studying and practicing them. If you practice according to this teaching, you will surely realize liberation."

When the Buddha finished giving this sutra, Venerable Sariputta stood up and bowed to the Buddha. All the other bhikkhus followed his example in order to show their deep gratitude to the Buddha. Venerable Sariputta announced to the community that there would be a special session to study the sutra the following day. He said that this sutra was immeasurably profound and they must devote their efforts to study, practice, and understand it. Venerable Svasti saw that this sutra was related to the Sutra on Emptiness which the Buddha had delivered the previous year. He saw how the Buddha was guiding his disciples from simple teachings towards ever more subtle and profound teachings. Svasti looked at the radiant and happy faces of such disciples as Mahakassapa, Sariputta, Punna, and Moggallana. Svasti remembered how the previous year they also followed Sariputta's example in bowing to the Buddha after he delivered the Sutra on Emptiness. He saw how deep the bond was between teacher and students.

The next afternoon, Venerables Yamelu and Tekula visited the Buddha at his hut. These two bhikkhus were brothers from the brahmana caste. They were well known for their expertise in linguistics and ancient literature. When they recited the scriptures, their voices were clear as bells and as resonant as drums. They bowed to the Buddha, and he invited them to be seated.

Venerable Yamelu spoke, "Lord, we would like to speak to you concerning the question of language as it relates to the dissemination of the teaching. Lord, you usually deliver your talks in Magadhi, but Magadhi is not the native tongue of many bhikkhus, and the people in some of the regions where the bhikkus teach do not understand Magadhi. Thus, they translate the teaching into local dialects. Before we were ordained, we had the good fortune to study many dialects and languages. It is our observation that the sublime and subtle nuances of your teaching have been hampered by being translated into local dialects and idioms. We would like your permission to render all your teachings into the classical meter of the Vedic language. If all the bhikkhus studied and taught the teaching in one language, distortion and error could be avoided."

The Buddha was silent for a moment. Then he said, "It would not be beneficial to follow your suggestion. The Dharma is a living reality. The words used to transmit it should be the words used daily by the people. I do not want the teaching to be transmitted in a language that can be understood by only a few scholars. Yamelu and Tekula, I want all my disciples, both ordained and lay, to study and practice the Dharma in their native tongues. That way the Dharma will remain vital and accessible. The Dharma must be applicable to present life, and compatible with local culture."

Understanding the Buddha's intent, Venerables Yamelu and Tekula bowed to him and took their leave.

CHAPTER TWENTY-FIVE

Where Will the Buddha Go?

One day during a rainstorm, an ascetic named Uttiya came to visit the Buddha. Ananda led him into the hut and introduced him to the Buddha. The ascetic was invited to sit down, and Ananda offered him a towel to dry himself.

Uttiya asked the Buddha, "Monk Gautama, is the world eternal or will it one day perish?"

The Buddha smiled and said, "Ascetic Uttiya, with your consent, I will not answer that question."

Uttiya then asked, "Is the world finite or infinite?"

"I will not answer that question either."

"Well then, are body and spirit one or two?"

"I will not answer that question either."

"After you die, will you continue to exist or not?"

"This question too, I will not answer."

"Or perhaps you hold that after death you will neither continue to exist nor cease to exist?"

"Ascetic Uttiya, I will not answer that question either."

Uttiya looked confounded. He said, "Monk Gautama, you have refused to answer every question I've asked. What question will you answer?"

The Buddha replied, "I only answer questions that pertain directly to the practice of gaining mastery over one's mind and body in order to overcome all sorrows and anxieties."

"How many people in the world do you think your teaching can save?" The Buddha sat silently. Ascetic Uttiya said no more.

Sensing that the ascetic felt that the Buddha didn't want to answer him, or was unable to, Ananda took pity on the man and spoke up, "Ascetic Uttiya, perhaps this example will help you better understand my teacher's intent. Imagine a king who dwells in a strongly fortified palace surrounded by a wide moat and wall. There is only one entrance and exit to the palace, which is guarded day and night. The vigilant guard will only allow persons he knows into the palace. No one else is granted permission to enter. The guard has furthermore made a careful check of the palace wall to make sure there are no gaps or cracks big enough for even a kitten to squeeze through. The king sits on his throne without concern for how many people enter the palace. He knows the guard will prevent all unwelcome guests from entering. It is similar for Monk Gautama. He is not concerned with the number of people who follow his Way. He is only concerned with teaching the Way, which has the capacity to dissolve greed, violence, and delusion, so that those who follow the Way can realize peace, joy, and liberation. Ask my teacher questions about how to master the mind and body, and he will surely answer you."

Ascetic Uttiya understood Ananda's example, but because he was still entangled in questions of a metaphysical nature, he asked no more. He departed feeling somewhat unsatisfied with his encounter with the Buddha.

A few days later, another ascetic, named Vacchagota, came to visit the Buddha. He asked the Buddha questions of a similar nature. For instance, he asked, "Monk Gautama, could you please tell me whether or not there is a self?"

The Buddha sat silently. He did not say a word. After asking several questions and receiving no reply, Vacchagota stood up and left. After he was gone, Venerable Ananda asked the Buddha, "Lord, you speak about the non-self in your Dharma talks. Why wouldn't you answer Vacchagota's questions about the self?"

The Buddha replied, "Ananda, the teaching on the emptiness of self is meant to guide our meditation. It is not to be taken as a doctrine. If people take it as a doctrine, they will become entangled by it. I have often said that the teaching should be considered as a raft used to cross to the other shore or a finger pointing to the moon. We should not become caught in the teaching. Ascetic Vacchagota wanted me to hand him a doctrine, but I do not want him to become trapped by any doctrine, whether it be a doctrine of the self or the non-self. If I told him there was a self, that would contradict my teaching. But if I told him there was no self, and he clings to that as a doctrine, it would not benefit him. It is better to remain silent than to answer such questions. It is better for people to think I do not know the answers to their questions than for them to become trapped in narrow views."

One day Venerable Anuradha was stopped by a group of ascetics. They did not want to let him pass until he answered their question. They asked him, "We have heard that Monk Gautama is a completely enlightened Master and that his teaching is subtle and profound. You are his disciple. Therefore, answer this—when Monk Gautama dies, will he continue to exist or will he cease to exist?"

The ascetics told Anuradha that he must select from one of the four following possibilities:

When he dies, Monk Gautama will continue to exist.

When he dies, Monk Gautama will cease to exist.

When he dies, Monk Gautama will both continue
to exist and cease to exist.

When he dies, Monk Gautama will neither continue
to exist nor cease to exist.

Bhikkhu Anuradha knew that none of these four responses was compatible with the true teaching. He remained silent. The ascetics did not want to accept his silence. They tried in vain to force him to select one of the four responses. At last, the Venerable said, "My friends, according to my understanding, none of these four responses can accurately express the truth concerning Monk Gautama."

The ascetics burst out laughing. One said, "This bhikkhu must be newly ordained. He doesn't possess the ability to answer our question. No wonder he's trying to avoid giving an answer. We'd better let him go."

A few days later, Venerable Anuradha presented the ascetics' question to the Buddha and said, "Lord, please enlighten us so that we can better answer such questions when they arise."

The Buddha said, "Anuradha, it is impossible to find Monk Gautama through conceptual knowledge. Where is Monk Gautama? Anuradha, can Gautama be found in form?"

"No, Lord."

"Can Gautama be found in feelings?"

"No, Lord."

"Can Gautama be found in perceptions, mental formations, or consciousness?"

"No, Lord."

"Well then, Anuradha, can Gautama be found outside of form?"

"No, Lord."

"Can Gautama be found outside of feelings?"

"No, Lord."

"Can Gautama be found outside of perceptions, mental formations, and consciousness?"

"No, Lord."

The Buddha looked at Anuradha. "Where then can you find Gautama? Anuradha, right this moment as you stand before Gautama, you cannot grab hold of him. How much less so after he dies! Anuradha, the essence of Gautama, like the essence of all dharmas, cannot be grasped by conceptual knowledge or in the categories of mental discrimination. One must see the dharmas in interdependent relation with all other dharmas. You must see Gautama in all the dharmas normally thought of as non-Gautama, in order to see the true face of Gautama.

"Anuradha, if you want to see the essence of a lotus flower, you must see the lotus present in all the dharmas normally thought of as non-lotus, such as the sun, pond water, clouds, mud, and heat. Only by looking in this way can we tear asunder the web of narrow views, which creates the prisons of birth and death; here and there; existence and non-existence; defiled and immaculate; and increasing and decreasing. It is the same if you want to see Gautama. The ascetics' four categories of existence, non-existence; both existence and non-existence; and neither existence nor non-existence, are spiderwebs among spiderwebs, which can never take hold of the enormous bird of reality.

"Anuradha, reality in itself cannot be expressed by conceptual knowledge or by written and spoken language. Only the understanding which meditation brings can help us recognize the essence of reality. Anuradha, a person who has never tasted a mango cannot know its taste no matter how many words and concepts someone else uses to describe it to him. We can only grasp reality through direct experience. That is why I have often told the bhikkhus not to lose themselves in useless discussion that wastes precious time better spent looking deeply at things.

"Anuradha, the nature of all dharmas is unconditioned and can be called suchness, or *tathata*. Suchness is the wondrous nature of all dharmas. From suchness the lotus arises. Anuradha arises from suchness. Gautama arises from suchness. We can call someone who arises from suchness a *tathagata*, or 'one who thus comes.' Arising from suchness, where do all dharmas return? All dharmas return to suchness. Returning to suchness can also be expressed by the term 'tathagata,' or 'one who thus goes.' In truth, dharmas do not arise from anywhere or go to any place, because their nature is already suchness. Anuradha, the truer meaning of suchness is 'one who comes from nowhere,' and 'one who goes nowhere.' Anuradha, from now on, I will call myself 'Tathagata.' I like this term because it avoids the discrimination that arises when one uses the words, 'I' and 'mine.'"

Anuradha smiled and said, "We know that all of us arise in suchness, but we will reserve the name 'Tathagata' for you.

Every time you refer to yourself as 'Tathagata,' we will be reminded how we all have the nature of suchness which has no beginning and no end."

The Buddha smiled too, and said, "The Tathagata is pleased with your suggestion, Anuradha."

Venerable Ananda was present at this conversation between the Buddha and Venerable Anuradha. He followed Anuradha out of the hut and suggested that they share the conversation with the rest of the community at the next day's Dharma discussion. Anuradha happily agreed. He said he would introduce the exchange by first recounting his meeting with the ascetics in Savatthi.

CHAPTER TWENTY-SIX

The Fruits of Practice

Just as the retreat season was ending, the sangha learned that war had broken out between Kosala and Magadha. Magadha's army, led by King Ajatasattu Videhiputta himself, had crossed over the Ganga into Kasi, a region under Kosala's jurisdiction. The king and his generals led an enormous battalion of elephants, horses, carts, artillery, and soldiers. Because it all happened so quickly, King Pasenadi was unable to inform the Buddha of his departure to Kasi. He asked Prince Jeta to explain the situation in his place.

The Buddha already knew that after King Pasenadi learned how Ajatasattu killed his own father to usurp the throne, King Pasenadi showed his opposition by reclaiming a district near Varanasi he had formerly presented to King Bimbisara. For nearly seventy years this district had brought in revenues of over a hundred thousand gold pieces to Magadha, and King Ajatasattu was not about to give it up. So he called his soldiers into battle.

Venerable Sariputta instructed all the bhikkhus and bhikkhunis to remain in Savatthi. It was too dangerous to travel with a war raging. He also asked the Buddha to remain in Savatthi until peace was restored.

Two months later, the people of Savatthi received the disheartening news that their army had suffered defeat in Kasi. King Pasenadi and his generals were forced to retreat back to the capital. The situation was fraught with tension, but thanks to a strong system of defense,

Savatthi did not fall, even though Ajatasattu's generals attacked day and night. Then, thanks to a brilliant plan devised by General Bandhula, King Pasenadi was able to mount a major counter-offensive. This time Kosala scored the decisive victory. King Ajatasattu and all his generals were captured alive. More than a thousand soldiers were taken prisoner. Another thousand had either been killed or fled. In addition, Kosala confiscated large numbers of elephants, horses, army carts, and supplies of artillery.

The war had raged for more than six months. The people of Savatthi organized a victory celebration. After dismantling his army, King Pasenadi visited the Buddha at Jetavana. He described the terrible cost of the war and said that Kosala had acted in self-defense when King Ajatasattu attacked their borders. He added that he believed King Ajatasattu had been wrongly influenced by his advisors.

"Lord Buddha, the king of Magadha is my own nephew. I cannot kill him, nor do I have any desire to put him in prison. Please help me find a wise course of action."

The Buddha said, "Your majesty, you are surrounded by loyal friends and aides. It is no surprise that you came out the victor in this war. King Ajatasattu is surrounded by bad elements and so he has gone astray. The Tathagata suggests you treat him with all the respect due a king of Magadha. Take time, as well, to guide him as your own nephew. Strongly impress on him the importance of surrounding himself with friends and aides of good and loyal character. Then you can send him back to Magadha with proper ceremony. The possibility of lasting peace depends on your skill in handling these matters."

The Buddha called for a young bhikkhu named Silavat and introduced him to King Pasenadi. Bhikkhu Silavat was originally a prince, one of King Bimbisara's sons, and King Ajatasattu's half-brother. Silavat was a wise and bright man who had studied the Dharma as a lay disciple under the guidance of Venerable Moggallana from the age of sixteen. After the changes that took place in Magadha, he asked Moggallana to allow him to be ordained, and he was sent to Jetavana in Savatthi to further his studies. Venerable Moggallana knew that although Silavat harbored no desire for the throne, it would nonetheless be safer for him to be out of King Ajatasattu's jealous reach.

King Pasenadi asked the young bhikkhu to describe the situation in Rajagaha. Silavat told the king all he had seen and heard before he left Magadha. He also informed the king that someone had been sent from Magadha to try and kill him, but he had been able to effect a change of heart in the assassin. That man was now an ordained bhikkhu himself living in a center close to the capital. King Pasenadi bowed to the Buddha and returned to his palace.

Shortly afterward, King Ajatasattu was released and allowed to return to Magadha. Using love to ease the wounds of hatred, King Pasenadi gave his own daughter, Princess Vajira, in marriage to Ajatasattu. Ajatasattu was now his son-in-law as well as his nephew. King Pasenadi also promised to return the district near Varanasi as a wedding gift. King Pasenadi had wholeheartedly followed the spirit of the Buddha's counsel.

With the war over, bhikkhus and bhikkhunis once again took to the road to spread the teaching. King Pasenadi ordered the construction of a new monastery on the outskirts of the capital and named it Rajakarama.

The Buddha remained in Kosala for the following two years, passing the retreat seasons at Jetavana and the rest of the time teaching throughout the region. From time to time he received news from Magadha from bhikkhus who had come from there. They told him that after the Buddha left Magadha, Venerable Devadatta ceased to enjoy the good graces of King Ajatasattu. Of the more than one hundred bhikkhus still with Devadatta at that time, eighty had returned to the Buddha's sangha at Bamboo Forest. Devadatta was more and more isolated. He had recently fallen ill and was unable to leave Gayasisa. Since the end of the war, King Ajatasattu had not paid him even one visit. King Ajatasattu did not pay any visits to Bamboo Forest either. He only maintained relations with leaders of other religious sects. Nonetheless, the sangha continued to spread the Dharma unimpeded.

The laity and bhikkhus in Magadha hoped that the Buddha would return to visit them. Vulture Peak and Bamboo Forest seemed empty without him. Jivaka awaited his return as well.

That winter, Queen Mallika of Kosala died. Deeply grieved, King Pasenadi came to the Buddha for comfort. The queen had been his closest friend, and he loved her with all his heart. She was a faithful disciple of the Buddha, a radiant spirit who understood the deeper reaches of the Dharma. Even before the king met the Buddha, the queen had shared her understanding of the Way with him. The king recalled how one night he had a disturbing dream, which he feared was a warning that misfortune would befall him. Placing his faith in the brahmans, he asked them to sacrifice several animals in order to ask the gods for protection. The queen dissuaded him from doing so. She had often served as a close advisor to the king on political matters, helping him find solutions to problems that beset the country. She was one of the Buddha's most devoted lay disciples. Because she loved to study the Dharma, she built a Dharma discussion hall in a park with many beautiful *tinduka* trees. She often invited the Buddha and his senior disciples to give Dharma discourses and lead discussions there. She also opened the hall to leaders of other religious sects to use.

Suffering from the loss of his companion of more than forty years, the king came to the Buddha. As he sat quietly next to the Buddha, he felt peace slowly return to his heart. He had been following the Buddha's suggestion to spend more time meditating. The Buddha reminded him of their previous conversation in which they discussed the importance of living according to the teachings in order to create happiness for those around one. The Buddha encouraged the king to reform the system of justice and economics in the country. He said corporal punishment, torture, imprisonment, and execution were not effective means for stopping crime. Crime and violence were the natural result of hunger and poverty. The best way to assist the people and provide for their security was to concentrate on building a healthy economy. It was essential to provide food, seeds, and fertilizer to poor farmers until they could become self-sufficient and productive. Loans should be provided to small merchants; retirement funds should be set up for those no longer able to work; and the poor should be exempted from taxes. All manner of coercion and oppression against manual laborers must cease. People should be free to select their own jobs. Ample opportunities for training should be made available to help people master the trades they chose. The Buddha said that a correct economic policy should be based on voluntary participation.

Venerable Ananda was sitting close to the Buddha during this conversation with the king. He was thus able to preserve the Buddha's ideas on politics and economics in the Kutadanta Sutra.

Late one afternoon Ananda found the Buddha sitting outside the Visakha Dharma hall. His back was turned to the sun. Ananda found it curious. The Buddha was usually fond of watching the sun set. He asked the Buddha about it, and the Buddha replied that he was letting the sun warm his back. Ananda approached and began to massage the Buddha's back. He knelt down to massage his legs as well. As he massaged the Buddha's legs, he remarked, "Lord, I have been your attendant for the past fifteen years. I remember how firm your skin was in the past and how it had such a healthy glow. But now your skin is wrinkled and your leg muscles have grown soft. Why, I can count all your bones!"

The Buddha laughed. "If you live long enough, you grow old, Ananda. But my eyes and ears are as sharp as ever. Ananda, do you miss Vulture Peak and the groves at Bamboo Forest? Wouldn't you like to climb Vulture Peak again and watch the sun set?"

"Lord, if you would like to return to Vulture Peak, please let me accompany you."

That summer the Buddha returned to Magadha. He walked leisurely, breaking the long trek into several short trips. He stopped all along the way to visit sangha centers. He taught the bhikkhus at each center and delivered talks to the laity. He passed through the kingdoms of Sakya, Malla, Videha, and Vajji, before he at last crossed the Ganga into Magadha. Before going on to Rajagaha, he stopped to visit the sangha center in Nalanda.

Bamboo Forest and Vulture Peak were as beautiful as ever. People from the capital and neighboring villages came to see the Buddha in droves. Nearly a month passed before the Buddha was free to accept Jivaka's invitation to visit his Mango Grove. Jivaka had built a new Dharma hall in the grove that was large enough to seat one thousand bhikkhus.

While they sat outside his hut at the Mango Grove, the Buddha listened to Jivaka recount events that had taken place in the Buddha's absence. Queen Videhi, he was pleased to learn, had found inner peace. She devoted time to meditation and had become a vegetarian. King Ajatasattu, on the other hand, was suffering from extreme mental anguish. He was haunted by his father's death and his mind could find no ease. His nerves were constantly on edge, and he was afraid to sleep at night because of the terrible nightmares he suffered. Many doctors and high-ranking priests from the sects of Makkhali Gosala, Ajita Kosakambali, Pakudha Kaccayana, Nigantha Nataputta, and Sanjaya Belatthiputta, had been summoned to try to cure him. Each priest hoped to effect a cure so that their particular sect would receive special patronage, but not one of them was able to help the king.

One day the king ate dinner with his wife, their son Udayibhadda, and his mother, the former queen Videhi. Prince Udayibhadda was almost three years old. Because the king catered to his son's every whim, the prince was an unruly and spoiled child. The prince demanded his dog be allowed to sit at the table with them. Though such a thing was normally forbidden, the king gave in to his son's wish. Feeling somewhat embarrassed, he said to his mother, "It is unpleasant having a dog sitting at the table, isn't it, but what else can I do?"

Queen Videhi answered, "You love your son and so you have allowed him to bring his dog to the table. There is nothing unusual about that. Do you remember how your own father once swallowed pus from your hand because he loved you?"

Ajatasattu did not recall the incident and asked his mother to tell him what had happened.

The queen said, "One day your finger became red and swollen. A boil formed underneath your fingernail. It caused you so much pain, you cried and fretted all day and night. Your father was unable to sleep out of concern for you. He lifted you onto his pillow and placed your infected finger in his mouth. He sucked on it to help relieve the pain. He sucked on your finger throughout four days and nights until the boil broke. He then sucked out the pus. He did not dare remove your finger from his mouth to spit out the pus for fear you would feel more pain. And so he swallowed the pus while continuing to suck on your finger. From this story, you can see how deeply your father loved you. You love your own son and that is why you have allowed him to bring his dog to the table. I can understand that very well."

The king suddenly clutched his head in his two hands and ran from the room, leaving his meal uneaten. After that night, his mental state worsened. At last, Jivaka was summoned to take a look at the king. Jivaka listened to Ajatasattu recount all his woes and how no priest or brahman had been able to help him. Jivaka sat without saying a word. The king asked, "Jivaka, why don't you say anything?"

Jivaka responded, "There is only one thing to tell you. Teacher Gautama is the only person who can help you overcome the agony in your heart. Go to the Buddha for guidance."

The king did not speak for several minutes. Finally he muttered, "But I am sure Teacher Gautama hates me."

Jivaka disagreed. "Don't say such a thing. Teacher Gautama does not hate anyone. He was your father's teacher and closest friend. Going to him will be like going to your own father. See him and you will find inner peace. You will be able to restore all you have torn asunder. My ability to heal is not worth anything compared with the Buddha's ability to heal. He is not a medical physician but he is the king of all physicians. Some people call him the Medicine King."

The king agreed to think about it.

The Buddha remained at Vulture Peak for several months. He visited the sangha centers in the region and also agreed to spend a month at Jivaka's Mango Grove. It was there that Jivaka arranged for King Ajatasattu to meet with the Buddha. On a moonlit night, the king, seated on an elephant, proceeded to the grove accompanied by the royal family, his concubines, palace guards, and Queen Videhi. When they entered the grove, all was still. The king was seized with sudden panic. Jivaka had told him that the Buddha was dwelling in the grove with a thousand bhikkhus. If that was true, how could it be so quiet? Could it be a trick? Was Jivaka leading him to be ambushed? He turned to Jivaka and asked if this was all a plot in order for Jivaka to seek revenge. Jivaka laughed out loud. He pointed to the Dharma hall from which light was streaming through a round window.

Jivaka said, "The Buddha and all the bhikkhus are in there this very moment."

The king climbed down from his elephant and entered the hall, followed by his family and attendants. Jivaka pointed to a man sitting on a platform, his back supported against a pillar, and said, "There is the Buddha."

The king was deeply impressed by the attentive quiet. A thousand bhikkhus surrounded the Buddha in perfect silence. Not even a robe rustled. King Ajatasattu had only seen the Buddha a few times in his life, as he had never joined his father in attending the Buddha's regular Dharma talks.

The Buddha invited the king and royal family to be seated. The king bowed and then spoke, "Lord, I remember hearing you speak at the palace when I was a young boy. Tonight, I would like to ask you a question. What kinds of fruit does the spiritual life bear that hundreds, even thousands, abandon their homes to pursue it?"

The Buddha asked the king if he had ever asked any other teacher the same question. The king responded that he had, in fact, asked dozens of other teachers including Venerable Devadatta, but he had never received a satisfactory answer.

The Buddha said, "Your majesty, tonight the Tathagata will tell you the fruits which can be found in this teaching, fruits that can be enjoyed in this very moment, and fruits which can be reaped in the future. You need not seek lofty answers. Simply look and see these fruits as clearly as a mango held in your own hand.

"Your majesty, consider this example. A servant caters to all his master's whims and commands from sun up to sundown, until one day he asks himself, 'As my master and I are both human beings, why should I allow myself to be abused by him?' The servant decides to leave his life as a servant to enter the homeless life of a bhikkhu. He pursues a chaste, diligent, and mindful life. He eats but one meal a day, practices sitting and walking meditation, and expresses calm dignity in all his movements. He becomes a respected, virtuous monk. Knowing that he was formerly a servant, if you met him, would you call out to him and say, 'Here, fellow, I want you to serve me from sun up to sundown. Obey all my commands.'"

The king said, "No, Lord, I would not address him in such a way. I would respectfully greet him. I would make food offerings to him and assure that he received the full protection of the law afforded to monks."

The Buddha said, "Your majesty, that is the first fruit a bhikkhu reaps. He is liberated from racial, social, and caste prejudice. His human dignity is restored."

The king said, "Wonderful, Lord! Please tell me more."

The Buddha continued, "Your majesty, dignity is only the first fruit. A bhikkhu observes two hundred fifty precepts, which enable him to dwell in calm peace. People who do not observe precepts are more easily misguided. They may commit such crimes as lying, drunkenness, sexual misconduct, stealing, and even murder. They bring cruel punishment on their minds and bodies by acting this way. They may be arrested and put in jail by the police and government officials. A bhikkhu observes the precepts of not killing, not stealing, not engaging in sexual misconduct, not lying, and not using alcohol. In addition, he observes more than two hundred other precepts, which assure him a carefree life unknown to those who do not observe precepts. Precepts help prevent one from falling into error, thus assuring a carefree state.

That is another fruit of spiritual practice which can be enjoyed right in the present moment."

The king said, "Wonderful, Lord! Please tell me more."

The Buddha continued, "Your majesty, a bhikkhu owns no more than three robes and a begging bowl. He has no fear of losing his possessions or being robbed. He knows he will not be attacked in the night by people who want to steal his wealth. He is free to sleep alone in the forest beneath a tree, relaxed and without worries. Freedom from fear is a great happiness. That is another fruit of spiritual practice which can be enjoyed right in the present moment."

The king trembled and said, "Wonderful, Lord! Please tell me more."

The Buddha continued, "Your majesty, a bhikkhu lives simply. Though he eats only one meal a day, his bowl receives offerings from a thousand different homes. He does not chase after wealth or fame. He uses only what he needs and remains unattached to desires. Living in such carefree ease is a great happiness. That is another fruit of spiritual practice which can be enjoyed right in the present moment."

The king said, "Wonderful, Lord! Please tell me more."

The Buddha continued, "Your majesty, if you knew how to practice full awareness of breathing and how to meditate, you could experience the happiness of one who follows the path. It is the happiness that meditation brings. A bhikkhu observes the six sense organs and overcomes the five obstacles of the mind which are greed, hatred, ignorance, torpor, and doubt. He uses the full awareness of breathing to create joy and happiness that nourishes his mind and body and helps him to make progress on the path of enlightenment. The pleasant sensations which result from gratifying sense desires are no measure for the joy and happiness that meditation brings. The joy and happiness of meditation permeates mind and body; heals all anxiety, sorrow, and despair; and enables the practitioner to experience the wonders of life. Your majesty, that is one of the most important fruits of spiritual practice and one which can be enjoyed right in the present moment."

The king said, "Wonderful, Lord! Please tell me more."

The Buddha continued, "Your majesty, thanks to dwelling diligently in mindfulness and observing the precepts, the bhikkhu is able to build concentration, which he can use to illuminate all dharmas. Thanks to his penetrating illumination, he sees the selfless and impermanent nature of all dharmas. Thanks to seeing the selfless and impermanent nature of all dharmas, he is no longer entangled by any dharma. He can thus cut through the ropes of bondage which bind most people— the ropes of greed, hatred, desire, laziness, doubt, false views of self, extreme views, wrong views, distorted views, and views advocating unnecessary prohibitions. Cutting through all these ropes, the bhikkhu attains liberation and true freedom. Your majesty, liberation is a great happiness and one of the greatest fruits of spiritual practice. There are bhikkhus sitting here tonight who have attained that fruit. That fruit, your majesty, can be attained right here in this life."

The king exclaimed, "Wonderful, Lord! Please tell me more."

The Buddha continued, "Your majesty, thanks to illuminating and seeing deeply into the nature of all dharmas, a bhikkhu knows that all dharmas are neither produced nor destroyed, neither defiled nor immaculate, neither increasing nor decreasing, neither one nor many, neither coming nor going. Thanks to this understanding, a bhikkhu does not discriminate. He regards all dharmas with complete equanimity, without fear or worry. He rides the waves of birth and death in order to save all beings. He shows all beings the Way so they too can taste liberation, joy, and happiness. Your majesty, being able to help others free themselves from the maze of desire, hatred, and ignorance is a great happiness. Such happiness is a sublime fruit of spiritual practice, which begins to be realized in the present, and extends to the future. Your majesty, in all of his contacts, a bhikkhu remembers his responsibility to guide others on the path of virtue and liberation. Bhikkhus do not engage in partisan politics but they contribute to building peace, joy, and virtue in society. The fruits of his spiritual practice are not for the bhikkhu's sole enjoyment and benefit. They are the people's and country's inheritance."

The king stood up and joined his palms in deepest respect. He said, "Most sublime Teacher! Lord! By the use of simple words, you have shown me the light. You have helped me see the true value of the Dharma. Lord, you have rebuilt that which was in ruins, revealed that which was concealed, shown the way to one who was lost, and brought light into the darkness. Please, Lord, accept me as your disciple, as you accepted my parents in the past."

The king prostrated himself before the Buddha.

The Buddha nodded his acceptance. He asked Venerable Sariputta to teach the three refuges to the king and queen. After they recited them, the king said, "As it is late, please allow us to return to the palace. I have an early morning audience."

The Buddha nodded again.

The encounter between the Buddha and King Ajatasattu benefited all those present. The king's mental torment rapidly improved. That same night he dreamed he saw his father smiling at him, and he felt that all that had been torn asunder was now made whole again. The king's heart was transformed, bringing great joy to all his people.

After that, the king visited the Buddha often, on his own. He no longer came on an elephant, accompanied by royal guards. He climbed the stone steps carved into the mountain just as his father King Bimbisara had done so often in the past. In his private meetings with the Buddha, King Ajatasattu was able to reveal his heart and confess his past crimes. The Buddha treated him as though he were his own son. He counseled the king to surround himself with men of virtue.

At the end of the retreat season, Jivaka asked the Buddha to allow him to enter the homeless life as a bhikkhu. The Buddha accepted him, and gave him the Dharma name of Vimala Kondanna. Bhikkhu Vimala Kondanna was permitted to continue to stay at the Mango Grove. There were about two hundred bhikkhus already in residence there. With so many mature mango trees, the Mango Grove monastery was a very pleasant place to stay. Bhikkhu Vimala Kondanna continued to grow medicinal herbs for the community of bhikkhus.

CHAPTER TWENTY-SEVEN

Stars in Your Eyes

When the retreat season ended, the Buddha and Ananda traveled throughout Magadha. They stopped in many out-of-the-way places and at every local Dharma center, so the Buddha could offer teachings to both the bhikkhus and the laity. The Buddha frequently pointed out beautiful scenery to Venerable Ananda. The Buddha knew that because Ananda devoted such wholehearted attention to attending to the Buddha's needs, he sometimes forgot to enjoy the countryside around them.

Ananda had served as the Buddha's attendant for nearly twenty years. Thinking back over the years, he recalled how often the Buddha pointed to the landscape and exclaimed such things as, "Look how beautiful Vulture Peak is, Ananda!" or "Ananda, look how beautiful the plains of Saptapanni are!" Ananda fondly remembered the day the Buddha pointed to golden rice fields bordered by green grasses and suggested they use the same pattern to sew the bhikkhus' robes. Ananda saw that the Buddha knew how to truly enjoy beautiful things while never becoming caught by either the beautiful or ugly.

The following rainy season, the Buddha returned to Jetavana. Because King Pasenadi was on a journey, he did not see the Buddha until the retreat was half-over. Immediately after his arrival, he visited the Buddha and told him that he no longer liked to be confined to the palace. Now that he was advanced in years, he had delegated many of his royal tasks to trusted ministers so that he could travel with a small party. He wanted to see and enjoy the land of his own country and that of neighboring kingdoms. When he visited another country, he never expected a formal reception. He came as a simple pilgrim. His trips were also occasions to practice walking meditation. Leaving behind all thoughts and worries, he took leisurely steps while enjoying the countryside. He told the Buddha how much these trips refreshed his heart.

"Lord Buddha, I am seventy-eight years old, the same as you. I know that you also enjoy walking in beautiful places. But I'm afraid my travels do not serve others in the way your travels do. Wherever you go, you stop to teach and guide the people. You are like a shining light wherever you go."

The king confided to the Buddha a secret pain he carried in his heart. Seven years earlier when an attempted coup took place in the capital, he wrongly accused the commander in chief of the royal forces, General Bandhula, and had him executed. A few years later he learned that the general had not been involved. The king was overcome with regret. He did all he could to restore the general's good name and provided ample assistance to his widow. He also appointed the general's nephew, General Karayana, as the new commander in chief of the royal forces.

During the remainder of the retreat season, the king visited Jetavana every other day to attend Dharma talks and discussions, and sometimes simply to sit quietly by the Buddha's side. When the retreat season came to a close, the Buddha began traveling. The king, too, set out on another trip with a small traveling party.

The following year, the Buddha spent two weeks in Kuru after the retreat season. Then he followed the river down to Kosali, Varanasi, and Vesali before returning north.

One day while staying in Medalumpa, a small district in Sakya, the Buddha received an unexpected visit from King Pasenadi. It so happened that the king was traveling in the same region with Prince Vidudabha and General Karayana. The king learned from some local people that the Buddha was staying not far away in Medalumpa. As it was only a half day's journey from where the king was, he instructed General Karayana to drive their carriage there. There were three other carriages in their party. They left their carriages outside the park where the Buddha was dwelling, and the king and the general entered the park together. The king asked a bhikkhu where to find the Buddha's hut and the bhikkhu pointed to a small hut beneath a shady tree.

The door to the hut was closed. The king walked leisurely to the hut and, before knocking, cleared his throat. He removed his sword and crown and handed them to the general, requesting the general to take them back to the carriage and wait for him there. The door to the Buddha's hut opened. He was most happy to see the king and invited him in at once. Venerables Sariputta and Ananda were also there. They stood to greet the king.

The Buddha asked the king to be seated on the chair next to his own. Sariputta and Ananda stood behind the Buddha. To their surprise the king stood up again and then knelt down and kissed the Buddha's feet. Several times he said, "Lord, I am King Pasenadi of the kingdom of Kosala. I respectfully pay you homage."

The Buddha assisted the king back onto his chair and asked, "Your majesty, we are old, close friends. Why do you pay me such formal respects today?"

The king answered, "Lord, I am old. There are a number of things I wish to say to you before it is too late."

The Buddha regarded him kindly and said, "Please speak."

"Lord, I have total faith in you, the Enlightened One. I have total faith in the Dharma and in the Sangha. I have known many brahmans and practitioners of other sects. I have watched so many of them practice in an upright manner for ten, twenty, thirty, or even forty years, only to finally abandon their practice to return to a life of indulgence. But among your bhikkhus, I do not see anyone abandoning his practice.

"Lord, I have seen kings oppose other kings; generals plot against other generals; brahmans compete with other brahmans; wives berate husbands; children accuse their parents; brothers argue with brothers; and friends fight with friends. But I see the bhikkhus living in harmony, joy, and mutual respect. They live together like milk and water. Nowhere else have I witnessed such harmony.

"Lord, wherever I go, I see spiritual practitioners whose faces are lined with worry, anxiety, and hardship. But your bhikkhus look refreshed and happy, relaxed and carefree. Lord, all these things strengthen my faith in you and your teaching.

"Lord, I am a king from the warrior caste. It is within my power to order anyone's death or to condemn anyone to prison. Even so, during councils with my ministers, I am often interrupted. But in your sangha, even when a thousand bhikkhus are gathered, there is never so much as a murmur or the rustling of a single robe to disturb your speaking. That is marvelous, Lord. You do not need to wield a sword or threaten others with punishment to be paid absolute respect. Lord, this strengthens my faith in you and your teaching.

"Lord, I have watched famous scholars scheme together to come up with questions that will confound you. But when they meet with you and hear you expound the Dharma, their mouths fall open and they forget their useless questions. They express nothing but admiration for you. Lord, this also strengthens my faith in you and your teaching.

"Lord, there are two highly skilled horsemen named Isidatta and Purana who work in the palace. They receive their wages from me, but the respect they hold for me is nothing compared to the respect they hold for you. I once took them with me on one of my travels. We were caught in a storm one night and had to seek shelter in a tiny palm-leaf hut. For most of the night, the horsemen spoke about your teaching. When they finally went to sleep, they slept with their heads in the direction of Vulture Peak and their feet pointing to me! You don't give them any wages, Lord. But they regard you far more highly than they do me. This also strengthens my faith in you and your teaching.

"Lord, you came from the same warrior caste as me. We are both seventy-eight years old this year. I wanted to take this occasion to

When the retreat season came to a close, the Buddha began traveling.

express my gratitude for the deep friendship we have shared. With your permission, I will now take my leave."

"Please, your majesty," said the Buddha, "take good care of your health." He walked with the king to the door. When the Buddha turned back to Ananda and Sariputta, he saw them standing silently with their palms joined. He said, "Sariputta and Ananda, King Pasenadi has just expressed his innermost sentiments about the three gems. Please share these things with others to help them strengthen their own faith."

The next month, the Buddha returned south to Vulture Peak. Upon his arrival he received two sad announcements: King Pasenadi had died under disturbing circumstances, and Venerable Moggallana had been murdered by hostile ascetics, just outside Bamboo Forest.

King Pasenadi did not die peacefully in his palace in Savatthi. He died in Rajagaha in circumstances hardly befitting a king. After visiting the Buddha that day in Medalumpa, the king walked back to his carriage. He was surprised to find only one carriage instead of the four he had left there. His attendant informed him that General Karayana had forced the others to return to Savatthi. The general still held the king's crown and sword. He told Prince Vidudabha to return at once to Savatthi and claim the throne as his own. The general said King Pasenadi was too old and weak to reign any longer. The prince was unwilling, but when General Karayana threatened to usurp the throne himself, the prince felt he had no choice but to obey the general's wishes.

King Pasenadi headed straight to Rajagaha intending to ask his nephew and son-in-law, King Ajatasattu, for assistance. The king was too upset to eat anything along the way and only drank a small amount of water. When they reached Rajagaha it was too late to disturb the palace. The king and his attendant checked into a local inn. That night the king fell suddenly ill and died in his attendant's arms before help could be sought. The attendant sobbed inconsolably over his king's sorry fate. When King Ajatasattu learned what had happened in the morning, he sent for King Pasenadi's body and ordered a solemn and majestic funeral be organized. When the funeral was over, he wanted to send soldiers to topple King Vidudabha, but he was discouraged by Bhikkhu Vimala Kondanna, formerly the physician Jivaka, who said that as King Pasenadi had already passed away and the new king was a rightful heir, there was no point in starting a war. Heeding this counsel. King Ajatasattu sent an envoy to Savatthi to express his recognition of the new king.

Venerable Moggallana was one of the Buddha's finest senior disciples, ranking with Sariputta and Kondanna. Many senior disciples had already passed away, including Kondanna, who had been among the Buddha's first five disciples. The Kassapa brothers had all died, and so had Abbess Mahapajapati. Bhikkhu Rahula had died at the age of fifty-one, shortly after his mother, Bhikkhuni Yasodhara died.

Venerable Moggallana was known for his fearless, upright character. He always spoke the truth directly and without compromise. Because of that, he had earned the hatred of others outside the sangha. The day of his death, he set out, accompanied by two disciples, quite early in the morning. Assassins were hiding just outside the monastery, waiting for him. When he appeared, they rushed out and began to beat him and the other two bhikkhus with large sticks. The bhikkhus were outnumbered and unable to defend themselves from the blows. Moggallana's two disciples were beaten and left by the side of the road. They cried out for help but it was too late. Venerable Moggallana let forth a cry that shook the forest. When other bhikkhus ran out of the monastery, Moggallana was dead and the assassins had disappeared.

Venerable Moggallana's body had already been cremated by the time the Buddha returned to Vulture Peak. An urn with his ashes had been placed just outside the Buddha's hut. The Buddha asked about Venerable Sariputta and was told that since Moggallana's murder, he had remained in his hut with the door closed. Sariputta and Moggallana had been like brothers, as close as a form and its shadow. The Buddha had not yet stopped to rest after his travels, but he proceeded at once to Sariputta's hut to console him.

As they walked to Sariputta's hut, Ananda reflected on how sad the Buddha must feel. How could he avoid feeling heartbroken when two of his closest friends had just died? The Buddha would console Sariputta, but who would console the Buddha? As if to answer Ananda's hidden thoughts, the Buddha stopped, looked at him, and said, "Ananda, everyone commends you for studying hard and possessing a phenomenal memory, but don't think that is enough. It is important to look after the Tathagata and the sangha, but it is not sufficient. Whatever time remains, devote your efforts to breaking through birth and death. Learn to look at birth and death as mere illusions, like the stars one sees in one's eyes after rubbing them."

Venerable Ananda bowed his head and continued walking in silence.

CHAPTER TWENTY-EIGHT

Be Diligent!

It was dusk by the time the Buddha and the bhikkhus reached the forest of sal trees. The Buddha asked Ananda to prepare a place between two sal trees for him to lie down. The Buddha lay on his side, his head facing north. All the bhikkhus sat around him. They knew that the Buddha would pass into nirvana that same night.

The Buddha looked up at the trees and said, "Ananda, look! It is not yet spring, but the sal trees are covered with red blossoms. Do you see the petals falling on the Tathagata's robes and the robes of all the bhikkhus? This forest is truly beautiful. Do you see the western horizon all aglow from the setting sun? Do you hear the gentle breeze rustling in the sal branches? The Tathagata finds all these things lovely and touching. Bhikkhus, if you want to please me, if you want to express your respect and gratitude to the Tathagata, there is only one way, and that is by living the teaching."

The evening was warm and Venerable Upavana stood over the Buddha to fan him, but the Buddha asked him not to. Perhaps the Buddha did not want his splendid view of the setting sun obstructed.

The Buddha asked Venerable Anuruddha, "I do not see Ananda, where is he?"

Another bhikkhu spoke up, "I saw brother Ananda standing behind some trees weeping. He was saying to himself, I have not yet attained my spiritual goal and now my teacher is dying. Who has ever cared more deeply for me than my teacher?'"

The Buddha asked the bhikkhu to summon Ananda. The Buddha tried to comfort Ananda. He said, "Don't be so sad, Ananda. The Tathagata has often reminded you that all dharmas are impermanent. With birth, there is death; with arising, there is dissolving; with coming together, there is separation. How can there be birth without death? How can there be arising without dissolving? How can there be coming together without separation? Ananda, you have cared for me with all your heart for many years. You have devoted all your efforts to helping me and I am most grateful to you. Your merit is great, Ananda, but you can go even farther. If you make just a little more effort, you can overcome birth and death. You can attain freedom and transcend every sorrow. I know you can do that, and that is what would make me the most happy."

Turning to the other bhikkhus, the Buddha said, "No one has been as good an attendant as Ananda. Other attendants in the past sometimes dropped my robe or bowl to the ground, but never Ananda. He has taken care of all my needs from the tiniest detail to the largest tasks. Ananda always knew when and where a bhikkhu, bhikkhuni, lay disciple, king, official, or practitioner from a different religious sect, should meet with me. He arranged all meetings most effectively and intelligently. The Tathagata believes that no enlightened master in the past or future could have an attendant more talented and devoted than Ananda."

Venerable Ananda wiped his tears and said, "Lord, please don't pass away here. Kusinara is just a small town of mud dwellings. There are so many more worthy places like Sampa, Rajagaha, Savatthi, Saketa, Kosambi, or Varanasi. Please Lord, select such a place to pass away so that more people will have a chance to see your face one last time."

The Buddha replied, "Ananda, Kusinara is also important, even if it is no more than a small town of mud dwellings.

The Tathagata finds this forest most agreeable. Ananda, do you see the sal flowers falling about me?"

The Buddha asked Ananda to go into Kusinara and announce to

*For six days and nights, the people of Kusinara came to the sal forest
to offer flowers, incense, dance, and music to the Buddha.*

the Mallas that the Buddha would pass into nirvana in the grove of sal trees at the night's last watch. When the Malla people heard this news, they hastily made their way to the forest. An ascetic named Subhadda was among them. While the people took turns bowing to the Buddha, Subhadda asked Venerable Ananda if he could have an audience with the Buddha. Ananda refused, saying the Buddha was too tired to receive anyone. But the Buddha overheard their conversation and said, "Ananda, let ascetic Subhadda speak with me. The Tathagata will receive him."

Ascetic Subhadda knelt before the Buddha. He had long felt drawn to the Buddha's teaching but had never met him before. He bowed and said, "Lord, I have heard about spiritual leaders such as Purana Kassapa, Makhali Gosala, Ajita Kesakambali, Pakudha Kaccayana, Sanjaya Belatthiputta, and Nigantha Nataputta. I would like to ask if, according to you, any of them attained true enlightenment."

The Buddha answered, "Subhadda, whether or not they attained enlightenment is not a necessary thing to discuss now. Subhadda, the Tathagata will show you the path by which you yourself can attain enlightenment."

The Buddha spoke to Subhadda about the Noble Eightfold Path. He concluded by saying, "Subhadda, wherever the Noble Eightfold Path is truly practiced, you will find people who have attained enlightenment. Subhadda, if you follow this path, you too can attain enlightenment."

Ascetic Subhadda felt his heart suddenly opened. He was filled with great happiness. He asked the Buddha to accept him as a bhikkhu. The Buddha asked the Venerable Anuruddha to perform the ordination ceremony right then and there. Subhadda was the last disciple received by the Buddha.

After Subhadda's head was shaved, he received the precepts and was given a robe and bowl. The Buddha then looked at all the bhikkhus sitting around him. Many bhikkhus from the vicinity had arrived and so there were now nearly five hundred. The Buddha spoke to them.

"Bhikkhus! If you have any doubts or perplexity concerning the teaching, now is the time to ask the Tathagata about it. Don't let this opportunity pass by, so that later you will reproach yourselves, saying, 'That day I was face to face with the Buddha, but I did not ask him.'"

The Buddha repeated these words three times, but no bhikkhu spoke.

Venerable Ananda exclaimed, "Lord, it is truly wonderful! I have faith in the community of bhikkhus. I have faith in the sangha. Everyone has clearly understood your teaching. No one has any doubts or perplexity about your teaching and the path to realize it."

The Buddha said, "Ananda, you speak from faith, while the Tathagata has direct knowledge. The Tathagata knows that all the bhikkhus here possess deep faith in the Three Gems. Even the lowest attainment among these bhikkhus is that of Stream-Enterer."

The Buddha looked quietly over the community and then said, "Bhikkhus, listen to what the Tathagata now says. Dharmas are impermanent. If there is birth, there is death. Be diligent in your efforts to attain liberation!"

The Buddha closed his eyes. He had spoken his last words. The earth shook. Sal blossoms fell like rain. Everyone felt their minds and bodies tremble. They knew the Buddha had passed into nirvana.

The Buddha had passed away. Some bhikkhus threw up their arms and flung themselves on the ground. They wailed, "The Buddha has passed away! The Lord has died! The eyes of the world are no more! Who can we take refuge in now?"

While these bhikkhus cried and thrashed about, other bhikkhus sat silently, observing their breath and contemplating the things the Buddha had taught them. Venerable Anuruddha spoke up, "Brothers, do not cry so pitifully! The Lord Buddha taught us that with birth there is death; with arising there is dissolving; with coming together there is separation. If you understand and follow the Buddha's teaching, you will cease to make such a disturbance. Please sit up again and follow your breathing. We will maintain silence."

Everyone returned to his place and followed Venerable Anuruddha's counsel. He led them in reciting sutras they all knew by heart, which spoke about impermanence, emptiness of self, non-attachment, and liberation. Calm dignity was restored.

The Mallas lit torches. Sounds of chanting echoed impressively in the dark night as everyone placed his full awareness on the words in the sutras. After a lengthy recitation, Venerable Anuruddha gave a Dharma talk. He praised the Buddha's attainments—his wisdom, compassion, virtue, concentration, joy, and equanimity. When Venerable Anuruddha finished speaking, Venerable Ananda recounted beautiful episodes from the Buddha's life. Throughout the night, the two venerables took turns speaking. The five hundred bhikkhus and three hundred lay disciples listened quietly. As torches burned down, new ones were lit to take their places until dawn broke.

CHAPTER TWENTY-NINE

Old Path White Clouds

When day broke. Venerable Anuruddha said to Venerable Ananda, "Brother, go into Kusinara and inform the authorities that our Master has passed away so that they may begin the necessary arrangements."

Venerable Ananda put on his outer robe and entered town. The Malla officials were holding a meeting to discuss local matters. When they learned the Buddha had passed away they expressed deep sorrow and regret. They put aside all other work in order to make arrangements for the Buddha's funeral. By the time the sun was perched above the trees, everyone in Kusinara knew of the Buddha's death in the forest of sal trees. Many beat their chests and sobbed. They regretted that they had not been able to look upon and bow to the Buddha before his death. People came to the forest bearing flowers, incense, musical instruments, and cloth streamers. They prostrated and placed flowers and incense around his body. They performed special songs and dances, and draped colorful streamers throughout the forest. People brought food offerings to the five hundred bhikkhus. Before long the sal forest had the atmosphere of a festival. Occasionally, Venerable Anuruddha invited the sound of the large bell to call people back to silence. He then led everyone in reciting passages from the sutras.

For six days and nights, the people of Kusinara and nearby Pava came to offer flowers, incense, dance, and music. Mandarava blossoms and other flowers soon thickly carpeted the area between the two sal trees. On the seventh day the Malla authorities bathed themselves in water perfumed with incense, put on ceremonial garments, and carried the Buddha's body into town. They passed through the town's center and out the east gate to Makuta-Bandhana temple, the main temple of the Mallas.

The town officials had planned a funeral fit for a king. The Buddha's body was wrapped in many layers of cloth and then placed in an iron coffin which was placed in another, larger iron coffin. It was then placed on a great funeral pyre of fragrant wood.

The moment to light the pyre had come. Just as the authorities approached with their torches, a messenger on horseback rode up and asked them to wait. He informed them that Venerable Mahakassapa and five hundred bhikkhus were on their way to the funeral from Pava.

Venerable Mahakassapa had been teaching the Dharma in Campa. He learned of the Buddha's imminent death in Vesali and that the Buddha was traveling north. The Venerable immediately set out to find the Buddha. Everywhere he went, other bhikkhus asked to join him. By the time he reached Bhandagama, there were five himdred bhikkhus with him. When they reached Pava, they met a traveler coming from the opposite direction with a sal flower tucked in his shirt. The man informed them that the Buddha had already passed away in the sal forest near Kusinara six days earlier. With that news, Mahakassapa's search came to an end, and he led his bhikkhus toward Kusinara. They met a man on horseback who agreed to gallop ahead to inform Venerable Anuruddha that they were on their way to attend the funeral.

At noon, Venerable Mahakassapa and the five hundred bhikkhus reached Makuta-Bandhana temple. The Venerable placed the end of his robe over his right shoulder, joined his palms and solemnly walked around the altar three times. He faced the Buddha and prostrated along with the five hundred bhikkhus. After they completed their third bow, the pyre was lit. Everyone, bhikkhus and laity alike, knelt down and joined their palms. Venerable Anuruddha invited the bell to sound and led everyone in reciting passages on impermanence, emptiness of self, non-attachment, and liberation. It was a most majestic sound. When the fire died down, perfume was poured over the ashes. The coffin was lowered and opened up, and the authorities placed the Buddha's relics into a golden jar, which was placed on the temple's main altar. Senior disciples took turns guarding the relics. News of the Buddha's death had been sent several days earlier to other cities, and delegations from neighboring kingdoms arrived to pay their respects. They were given a share of the Buddha's relics to be kept in stupas. There were representatives from Magadha, Vesali, Sakya, Koliya, Bulaya, Pava, and Vetha. They divided the relics into eight portions. The people of Magadha would build a stupa in Rajagaha; the people of Licchavi would build one in Vesali; the people of Sakya would build one in Kapilavatthu; the Buli people in Allakappa; the Koliya people in Ramagama; the Vetha people in Vethadipa; and the Mallas in both Kusinara and Pava.

After the delegations returned to their own countries, all the bhikkhus returned to their own locales to practice and teach. Venerables Mahakassapa, Anuruddha, and Ananda brought the Buddha's begging bowl back to Bamboo Forest.

A month later, Venerable Mahakassapa organized an assembly of bhikkhus in Rajagaha with the purpose of compiling all the sutras and precepts that the Buddha had given them. Five hundred bhikkhus were to be selected based on their standing and experience in the sangha. The assembly was to begin at the beginning of the retreat season and last for six months.

Venerable Mahakassapa had been considered the fourth highest-ranking disciple of the Buddha after Venerables Kondanna, Sariputta, and Moggallana. He was especially regarded for his simple living and humility. He had been deeply trusted and loved by the Buddha. Everyone in the sangha had heard about the time twenty years earlier when Mahakassapa sewed his own sanghati from several hundred scraps of discarded cloth. Once he folded this sanghati and invited the Buddha to sit upon it. The Buddha remarked how soft a cushion it made and Venerable Mahakassapa offered the robe to the Buddha. The Buddha accepted it with a smile and offered his own sanghati to Mahakassapa in return. Everyone also knew that Mahakassapa was the one monk who smiled the time the Buddha silently lifted up a lotus flower at Jetavana. Mahakassapa had thus received the Buddha's transmission of the Dharma treasure.

King Ajatasattu sponsored the assembly. Because Venerable Upali was highly regarded for his thorough knowledge of the precepts, he was invited to recite them all for the assembly, as well as recount the specific conditions and situations that gave rise to each of the precepts. Venerable Ananda was to be invited to repeat all of the Buddha's Dharma talks, including the details concerning the time, place, and situation that gave rise to each talk.

Naturally, Venerables Upali and Ananda could not be expected to remember every detail, and so the presence of five hundred respected bhikkhus was of great help. During the special gathering, all the precepts were compiled and given the name Vinaya pitaka, the basket of discipline. The basket of compiled Dharma talks was named Sutra pitaka. The sutras were divided into four categories, based on their length and subject matter. Venerable Ananda shared with the assembly that the Buddha had told him that after the Buddha's death, they could discard the lesser precepts. The other bhikkhus asked Ananda whether the Buddha had stated clearly which precepts he meant, but Ananda admitted he had not thought of asking the Buddha that question. After lengthy discussion, the bhikkhus decided to preserve all the precepts for both bhikkhus and bhikkhunis.

Remembering the Buddha's words, they agreed not to render the sutras into the classical meter of the Vedic language.

Ardhamagadhi was the primary language the sutras and precepts had been given in. The assembly agreed to encourage the translation of the sutras into other languages to enable people to study them in their native tongues. They also decided to increase the number of bhikkhus whose role it was to recite the sutras in order to transmit them for both present and future generations.

When the assembly adjourned, all the bhikkhus returned to their own places of practice and teaching.

Venerable Svasti watched the young buffalo boys cross the Neranjara River.

Afterword

Along the banks of the Neranjara River, Venerable Svasti stood to watch the flowing waters. Young buffalo boys on the opposite shore were preparing to lead their buffaloes across the shallow river. Each boy carried a sickle and a basket, just as Svasti had done forty-five years earlier. He knew that the boys would fill their baskets with fresh kusa grass while the buffaloes grazed.

The Buddha had bathed in this same river. There was the bodhi tree, more green and healthy than ever. Venerable Svasti slept beneath that beloved tree during the night. The forest was no longer the place of solitude it had once been. The bodhi tree was now a place where pilgrims visited, and much of the forest had been cleared of brush and thorns.

Venerable Svasti felt grateful that he had been one of the five hundred bhikkhus invited to attend the assembly. He was now fifty-six years old. His closest friend on the path, Venerable Rahula, had died five years earlier. Rahula had been an embodiment of devoted and diligent effort. Though he was the son of royalty, he lived in utmost simplicity. He was a modest man, and though his accomplishments in spreading the teaching were great, he never spoke about them.

Venerable Svasti had been with the Buddha on his last journey from Rajagaha to Kusinara. He was present during the final hours of the Buddha's life. On the road from Pava to Kusinara, Svasti remembered how Venerable Ananda asked the Buddha where he was heading. The

Buddha simply said, "I'm heading north." Svasti felt he understood. Throughout his life, the Buddha had traveled without thinking about his destination. He had taken each step mindfully, enjoying the present moment. Like an elephant prince returning to its native land when it knows its time has come, the Buddha headed north in the last days of his life. He didn't need to reach Kapilavatthu or Lumbini before he passed into nirvana. To head north was sufficient. Kusinara itself was the Lumbini Gardens.

Drawn homeward in a similar way, Venerable Svasti had returned to the banks of the Neranjara the night before. This was his own home. He still felt like the eleven-year-old who tended another man's buffaloes to feed his younger siblings. Uruvela village was the same as ever. Papaya trees still grew before every house. The rice fields were still there; the gentle river flowed as before. Water buffalos were still led and bathed by young buffalo boys. Though Sujata no longer lived in the village and his own siblings had started families of their own and moved away, Uruvela would always be Svasti's home. Svasti thought back to the first time he saw the young monk Siddhartha doing walking meditation in the forest. He thought of the many meals the village children had shared with Siddhartha beneath the cool shade of the pippala tree. These images of the past could live again. When the buffalo boys crossed over to his side, he would introduce himself. Every one of those boys was Svasti. Just as long ago he had been given a chance to enter the path of peace, joy, and liberation, he would show the path to these young boys.

Venerable Svasti smiled. A month earlier in Kusinara, he had listened to Venerable Mahakassapa tell about an encounter he had with a young bhikkhu named Subhada who traveled with him from Pava. When Subhada learned that the Buddha had already passed away, he remarked glibly, "The old man is gone. From now on, we are free. No one will scold or reproach us anymore." Venerable Mahakassapa was shocked at the young bhikkhu's foolish comment, but he did not say anything.

Venerable Mahakassapa did not scold the young Subhada, but he did not mince words with Venerable Ananda, even though Ananda was a deeply respected senior disciple. Venerable Ananda's presence at the assembly was considered essential in order to accurately compile all the sutras. Nonetheless, just three days prior to the assembly, Venerable Mahakassapa told Venerable Ananda that he was seriously considering barring Ananda from the gathering. The reason he gave was that although Venerable Ananda had a solid grasp of the teaching, he had not yet attained true realization. The other bhikkhus feared Ananda would be insulted by Mahakassapa's comments and perhaps even leave, but Ananda simply retired to his own hut and closed the door. He remained there three days and nights deep in meditation. Just before dawn on the day of the assembly, Venerable Ananda attained the Great Awakening. After practicing sitting meditation all night long, he finally decided to rest. As his back touched his sleeping mat, he attained enlightenment.

That morning when Venerable Mahakassapa met Venerable Ananda, he looked into Ananda's eyes and knew at once what had happened. He told Ananda he would see him at the assembly.

Svasti looked up and saw the white clouds floating across the blue sky. The sun had risen high, and the green grass along the riverbanks sparkled in the morning light. The Buddha had walked on this very path many times as he traveled to Varanasi, Savatthi, Rajagaha, and countless other places. The Buddha's footprints were everywhere, and with each mindful step, Svasti knew he was walking in the footsteps of the Buddha. The Buddha's path was at his feet. The same clouds the Buddha had seen were in the sky. Each serene step brought to life the old path and white clouds of the Buddha. The path of the Buddha was beneath his very feet.

The Buddha had passed away, but Venerable Svasti could see his presence everywhere. Bodhi seeds had been planted throughout the Ganga basin. They had taken root and given rise to healthy trees. No one had heard of the Buddha or the Way of Awakening forty-five years before. Now saffron-robed monks and nuns were a common sight. Many Dharma centers had been established. Kings and their families had taken the refuges, as had scholars and officials. The poorest and most oppressed members of society had found refuge in the Way of Awakening. They had found liberation for their lives and spirits in the Way. Forty-five years before, Svasti was a poor, untouchable buffalo boy. Today he was a bhikkhu who had transcended all the barriers of caste and prejudice. Venerable Svasti had been greeted respectfully by kings.

Who was the Buddha that he had been able to effect such profound change? Venerable Svasti asked himself that question as he watched the buffalo boys busily cutting kusa grass along the shore. Though many of the Buddha's senior disciples had passed away, there remained bhikkhus of great effort and attainment. Many of these monks were still young. The Buddha was like the seed of a mighty bodhi tree. The seed had cracked open in order for strong roots to take hold in the earth. Perhaps when people looked at the tree, they no longer saw the seed, but the seed was there. It had not perished. It had become the tree itself. The Buddha taught that nothing passes from existence to non-existence. The Buddha had changed form, but he was still present. Anyone who looked deeply could see the Buddha within the sangha. They could see him in the presence of young bhikkhus who were diligent, kind, and wise. Venerable Svasti understood that he had a responsibility to nurture the Dharma body of the Buddha. The Dharma body was the teaching and the community. As long as the Dharma and the Sangha remained strong, the Buddha would remain present.

Venerable Svasti smiled as he watched the buffalo boys cross to his side of the river. If he didn't continue the Buddha's work by bringing equality, peace, and joy to these children, who would? The Buddha had initiated the work. His disciples would have to continue it. The bodhi seeds that the Buddha sowed would continue to put forth roots throughout the world. Venerable Svasti felt as if the Buddha had sown ten thousand precious seeds in the earth of his own heart. Svasti would tend those seeds carefully to help them grow into strong, healthy bodhi trees. People said that the Buddha had died; yet Svasti saw that the Buddha was more present than ever. He was present in Svasti's own mind and body. He was present everywhere Svasti looked—in the bodhi tree, the Neranjara River, the green grass, the white clouds, and the leaves. The young buffalo boys were themselves little Buddhas. In a moment, he would strike up a conversation with them. They too could continue the Buddha's work. Svasti understood that the way to continue the Buddha's work was to look at all things with awareness, to take peaceful steps, and to smile with compassion, as the Buddha had done.

The Buddha was the source. Venerable Svasti and the young buffalo boys were rivers that flowed from that source. Wherever the rivers flowed, the Buddha would be there.

Parallax Press, a nonprofit organization, publishes books on engaged Buddhism and the practice of mindfulness by Thich Nhat Hanh and other authors. All of Thich Nhat Hanh's work is available at our online store and in our free catalog. For a copy of the catalog, please contact:

Parallax Press
P.O. Box 7355
Berkeley, CA 94707
Tel: (510) 525-0101

Monastics and laypeople practice the art of mindful living in the tradition of Thich Nhat Hanh at retreat communities worldwide. To reach any of these communities, or for information about individuals and families joining for a practice period, please contact:

Plum Village
13 Martineau
33580 Dieulivol, France
www.plumvillage.org

Blue Cliff Monastery
3 Mindfulness Road
Pine Bush, NY 12566
www.bluecliffmonastery.org

Magnolia Grove Monastery
123 Towles Rd.
Batesville, MS 38606
www.magnoliagrovemonastery.org

Deer Park Monastery
2499 Melru Lane
Escondido, CA 92026
www.deerparkmonastery.org

The *Mindfulness Bell*, a journal of the art of mindful living in the tradition of Thich Nhat Hanh, is published three times a year by Plum Village. To subscribe or to see the worldwide directory of Sanghas, visit **www.mindfulnessbell.org**